Searching for Serenity

Other titles in this series, available from
Redemptorist Publications:

Finding Forgiveness: Personal and Spiritual Perspectives

The Inside Job: A Spirituality of True Self-Esteem

Searching for Serenity:
Spirituality in Later Life

Jim McManus C.Ss.R.
&
Stephanie Thornton

redemptorist
p u b l i c a t i o n s

Published by **Redemptorist Publications**
Alphonsus House, Chawton, Hampshire, GU34 3HQ UK
Tel. +44 (0)1420 88222, Fax +44 (0)1420 88805
email sales@rpbooks.co.uk, www.rpbooks.co.uk
A registered charity limited by guarantee
Registered in England 3261721

First published in October 2010
Second printing April 2011
Third printing January 2015

Layout and cover design by Peena Lad

ISBN 978-0-85231-380-0

A catalogue record for this book is available from the British Library.

Printed by Bishops Printers Limited, Portsmouth PO6 1TR

Acknowledgements

We'd like to thank the many men and women, some of whom are mentioned in the text, who have shared their human journey with us. We've learned a great deal through hearing their stories and their struggles, and through the privilege of sharing their experiences.

We'd also like to thank Routledge Mental Health for providing material in support of the research for this book; and Andrew Lyon, Editorial Manager at Redemptorist Publications, for his encouragement and support in writing it.

We dedicate this book to all those who long for the gift of serenity, all those who dare to reach out to find it –

and especially

to Lillian, and in memory of Thomas and Doty and Brian.

Contents

Preface

For many people, growing old is a difficult or even depressing experience. We come face to face with the frailties of our human bodies, the transience of our human concerns and the reality of our human mortality.

The challenge of ageing is a spiritual challenge. We can't turn back the clock and be young again! We must find ways to come to terms with the myriad of changes and challenges which come with later life. We two writing this book believe that this spiritual challenge can be the greatest adventure of our lives, and can bring us to the very special spiritual gift of serenity! *But how?* We invite you to share our exploration of that vital question.

This is a book of two parts, the one focusing primarily on our human experience of ageing, the other focusing on the words God speaks to us as we face that experience.

Each chapter begins by reflecting on some aspect of our human journey into later life, exploring the challenges and opportunities that it presents in our search for spiritual maturity and the peace and joy that is serenity. We will propose a meditative practice after each of these discussions. We hope that both our reflections and our meditative practices will speak to everyone, believer or not, Christian or not – for we all share the same spiritual challenges of ageing, and the gift of serenity is there for us all.

Each chapter ends with the invitation of Christ, looking very specifically at the word of God as it speaks to us in each of the challenges of later life. We hope that, believer or not, the invitation of Christ will touch your soul.

Jim McManus
Stephanie Thornton

St Mary's Monastery, Kinnoull, October 2009

1

Serenity, spiritual fulfilment and later life

"Be still, and know that I am God!"
Psalm 46:10

What is serenity? Why is it a good thing? What has it got to do with spiritual fulfilment? And what has that got to do with later life? Above all: *how can we find it?*

The challenge of later life

Leon Trotsky wrote: "Old age is the most unexpected of all the things that happen."[1] One minute we are busily engaged in the myriad of tasks which shape our adult lives, confident in our youth and vigour – our "prime" of life. The next minute – or so it seems – we are, if not actually old, then certainly aware that we are heading that way at a startling pace!

Becoming older challenges us on many levels. All sorts of things that we would like to hang on to for ever start slipping away: our responsibilities, our relationships, our looks, our vigour, our health, perhaps even our minds – and, eventually, life itself. And along the way our identity is deeply challenged: the roles we've held all these years, the connections and friendships and loves that have defined us, the work that has specified our place in society – our answer to the question *who am I?* changes. We seem to slip from centre stage to the wings, edging ever nearer to the darkness.

For many, perhaps for all of us at some time, ageing brings pain and fear. Everyday life gets harder, and we worry about coping with the practicalities as we become more frail and vulnerable. In the wee small hours we tend to reflect regretfully on our lives – the mistakes we think we've made, the griefs and grievances we've suffered. We reflect on what might have been; on the hopes and dreams that haven't been fulfilled; on the people we have loved who are gone. We wonder what it has all amounted to, now that it seems too late to change the history of our experience. And then, too, we begin to look forward anxiously to a future which suddenly seems too short. We begin to think about death – not just as an abstract thing that comes to someone else, or perhaps bears away some unfortunates, the way the odd glass is accidentally broken in everyday life – but as something as inevitable and inexorable as the sunset, something real that is coming for *me*; something that puts our courage, our confidence, even our faith to the test.

Where can we turn to find solace for the pains and fears of later life? Suddenly the true reality of the human condition comes home to us. No medicine or science can stop the flow of time or make us young again, or give us immortality in this world! The practical realities of ageing can be postponed to some extent, but can't, in the end, be avoided. More fundamentally, there is no material fix for the existential challenges of life, the questions of the meaning of life and death which have been there all along, but which take on a new significance and urgency as we age.

Sadly, many people find no solution to the challenges of ageing. They fight desperately to hang on to youth, denying and refusing to engage with the new realities of later life, viewing them only as enemies to be ignored or held at bay. Or worse, they opt out altogether and despair: we think of suicide as a phenomenon of youth, but it is most common in later life, and grows increasingly common as people pass from 60 to 90. In our society only the happy few find a better way through shifting their focus from the material to the spiritual: only the happy few grow to accept the reality of the human condition and, in the process, find serenity.

The nature of serenity

At some level all of us have some sort of idea what serenity is: it is "the peace... which surpasses all understanding" (Philippians 4:7). It is a pure peace that is the source of intense joy.

Peace is the sensation we feel when we have no worries. In the physical prime of our lives when we are young and strong, our anxieties tend to revolve around practical things – the challenges of everyday living, such as work and play, family and friends, dreams and ambitions. When things go well we may be at peace with the world, and even joyful. But for most of us this peace and joy have shallow foundations: they are rooted in material success or physical wellbeing, and don't survive adversity. Faced with a threat to our way of living we readily find our peace and joy shattered. This is not serenity.

Even in youth it is not always possible to overcome the adversities of the material world in practical ways and so restore peace and happiness. Even in youth we may be faced with existential challenges of life and death which can have no material solution. Even in youth we need a basis for peace and joy that can transcend the pains of life. But this need becomes urgent, obvious and inevitable as we age, as we face the final challenges of human life. As Hillel the Elder, a Jewish sage writing shortly before the birth of Christ, put it, the ageing face the question: *if not now, when?* Ageing presents us with the moment for dealing with reality.

As we age, the adversities we face are more and more of the kind that can't be reversed by some practical "cure"; more and more of the kind that pose existential rather than practical challenges. Peace and joy rooted in material success or physical vigour are revealed for what they are and always have been – security built on sand. Now, if we seek peace, we must find it in another, more lasting way, that can endure whatever adversity we may have to face, even the nearness of death. Peace of *this* kind, peace which survives, transcends all the woes of the material world – *this* is serenity: the conviction that "Even though I walk through the darkest valley" (Psalm 23:4) there is nothing to fear. As Julian of Norwich put it:

> All shall be well, and all shall be well,
> And all manner of things shall be well.[2]

Serenity and spiritual fulfilment

You don't have to be a great guru to realise that, for all its beauties, this human life is also beset with sorrows. Many people suffer a great deal one way or another through the course of a lifetime. And all of us must come to terms with the fact that everything we love most in this life is fragile, transient and ephemeral – including our very selves.

What is the point of a human life if it may be lived in suffering, and will necessarily end in death? Why are we here? How should we try to live? These are the questions at the core of the human mystery, which religion and philosophy set out to try to answer. For the believer and non-believer alike, these are *spiritual* questions: questions not about facts, but about *meaning* and *value*. They are questions about how to make sense of our experiences, for good or ill.

Different religions, philosophies and even science offer various answers to the puzzle of the origins and purpose of creation – our universe and all that is in it – the puzzle of how and why we are here. Their answers sometimes converge and are sometimes profoundly at odds with one another. But there is an astonishing degree of agreement across religions, philosophies and even science on the ideal human life: *it is a life which achieves a transcendental serenity.* For the greatest human thinkers from all sorts of backgrounds, this is the highest possible human achievement, the fulfilment of life's purpose. To achieve serenity is to achieve spiritual fulfilment. Why so?

For science and medicine a serene approach to life is, objectively, the healthiest way of being. Those who can achieve the calm detachment of serenity suffer far less stress and far less stress-related illness, physical and psychological, even though they may go through the same traumatic experiences as those who cannot share that peace. And serenity is not simply a matter of calm detachment: there is a pure joy that goes with the peace which surpasses all understanding, a glory in being alive that is the essence of happiness. Serenity is far more than the antidote to stress: it is the gift of life. Science tells us that those who can live in this *gratitude* and *confidence* live long and prosper: through serenity, the body achieves its full potential.

For religious people who do not believe in a personal god, such as Buddhists, serenity is far more than merely mental hygiene – as potent and valuable as that is. For Buddhists, serenity is nothing less than enlightenment – a state of profound understanding and insight, *awareness* which allows us to have a proper relationship with the world and with ourselves. The enlightened are serene because they have escaped the illusions of everyday life and entered a more profound relationship with reality – a relationship which is blissful because it wholly transcends the ephemera of wanting and desiring, ambition and control; blissful because it accepts that the world *just is*; blissful because this mindset escapes suffering; blissful because it embraces *the good*: the desire to do no harm, to do good without wanting to control the world! Here is a concept challenging to the Western mind – but all the more mysterious and seductive for that. Ancient wisdom tells us that those who can achieve this *mystical contemplation*, this *detachment,* are filled with peace and moral joy. Through serenity / enlightenment, human consciousness achieves its full potential.

For those who believe in God, as Jews, Christians, Muslims and others do, the state of serenity brings with it all the virtues of mental hygiene that science acknowledges, and all the virtues of contemplative enlightenment that non-theistic religion understands. But it also carries a crucial extra dimension: this is the dimension of connection, union, solidarity – the dimension that is the foundation of love. For the believer, the gratitude and trust, mystical contemplation and awareness that are the heart of serenity connect us with something that far transcends individuality, something far greater than we are. Many who are not believers will know the feeling that there is something there, half understood, half felt. Many have a nebulous sensation of the sacredness of life, of the numinous. For the believer, the trust and calm, the detachment and awareness of serenity create the space in which we can connect directly to the pervading presence in the universe that we call God. Spiritual fulfilment indeed! And from the awe, the power and joy of this connection comes overflowing love, a transcendent connection, not only to God, but in solidarity and union with all people, with all creation, with ourselves. The great prayer of the Jewish prophets, of the Muslim mystics, of the Christian saints has always been for the grace to find and live in this peace of God, the peace which surpasses all understanding, and to share it with others:

> Drop thy still dews of quietness,
> till all our strivings cease;
> take from our souls the strain and stress,
> and let our ordered lives confess
> the beauty of thy peace.
> The beauty of thy peace.[3]

Serenity, spirituality and human development over 60

It's never too soon to search for serenity. All the great religions of the world urge us to do this from our earliest youth! But until we reach the maturity of later life, most of us are too bound up in the challenges and opportunities of the material world – too focused on establishing ourselves in that world, too confident in our health and vigour with what seems like an endless horizon stretching before us, to really understand either the need for, or the nature of, transcendental serenity.

If the first journey of life, the journey of youth, is the *practical* journey – the journey to find happiness in material success – then the search for serenity that can transcend the fragility and pain of life is the second journey – the *spiritual* journey. And although we could embark on that second journey any time we choose, most of us in our privileged Western society are only mature enough, only confronted with the compelling need to take that second journey, later in life, when the troubles of ageing begin to mount up.

Many people think of those in later life as being "over the hill" – winding down in life. Seen through the eyes of youth, later life is indeed a period of loss: the loss of looks and vigour, sensuality and strength, health of the body and possibly the mind that has defined our sense of self. It is also a period when we lose the roles and careers which have defined our adult identity; it's the time when parents are left with an "empty nest", as the next generation moves into independent adult life. These and other common losses of ageing are the triggers which start many people wondering what life is all about and how to meet the existential challenges of ageing and death. Many people face these losses with regret or even despair. But psychologists such as Judith Viorst argue that they are the *necessary* losses of later life, propelling us towards the later stages of human development, which are the pinnacle of our human journey.[4] For human development does not end at 60! In fact, *it's not over till it's over.*

The necessary losses of ageing present us with a challenge, a developmental task. We must move on from the physical beauty of youth to find self-esteem – a way of connecting to others which transcends the ageing of the body. We must move on from an identity defined by a job or role to find identity in our character, which is defined by *being* rather than *doing.* We must acknowledge unfulfilled hopes and dreams and find a way to love the reality of the life we are actually living. And, above all, we must give up the childish illusion that we can fix things the way we want them to be – and find maturity in facing the uncertainties of ageing and the certainty of death. These are human tasks, the final challenges of human development. But the challenge they present is spiritual: no less than the challenge to find a transcendental serenity, a serenity rooted in meaning and value that can survive the necessary losses of ageing! The later stages of human development are a human journey with a spiritual destination in serenity.

Searching for serenity
There's a sense in which serenity is always the gift of God: something we can only pray for. But it takes grace to receive a gift with acceptance

and gratitude. Above all, embracing a gift requires awareness: an appreciation of the value of what is given. And true acceptance, truly taking a gift to our heart, requires the belief that we *deserve* this gift, and have the *right* to embrace it.

The gift of serenity is there for us all – believer or unbeliever, man or woman, old or young. We have only to be open to receiving it. And that's what this book is about: how we can work to embrace the gift of serenity, especially as we age.

About this book

Ageing takes us out of our human comfort zone. We don't really want to face the necessary losses and developmental challenges of later life – in other words, we don't really want to face the realities of the human condition! And whereas, in the earlier stages of life, society is quite clear about what we ought to be doing, how we ought to develop, how we ought to cope, there is remarkably little advice on development after 60 and retirement. Ageing can be a lonely and puzzling time.

And yet the two of us writing this book believe that the challenges of later life, and the spiritual journey that they open up for us, are full of possibilities that make later life potentially the most exciting and fulfilling time of life!

Each chapter presents a reflection on an aspect of being human, and its significance for us in our search for spiritual meaning and serenity. We hope that, together, they amount to a whole picture of the path to serenity through our lived experience, especially in later life. Much about the human experience and spiritual development is common to us all – insights shared across all religions and cultures, equally valid for believer and non-believer and, in truth, for the young as much as the old. We hope that, whatever your beliefs or doubts, you will take encouragement from exploring with us the trials and tribulations of the human condition, and the gifts of living a long life.

We are Catholic, and we will share our Christian perspective with you. You are free to embrace or reject our beliefs, but we hope you will understand them. But whether you share our faith or not, we hope that you will come to share our conviction that serenity is the fulfilment of human potential – and available to us all.

A child on the edge of adult life hesitates on the threshold every bit as much as we in later life hesitate to let go of the old familiar ways of our adult prime. Just as the child must "put an end to childish ways" (1 Corinthians 13:11) to enter into adulthood, so we must let go of the habits of adult life to enter into full maturity. And just as the caterpillar can have little idea of the glory to come as it enters into its dark cocoon, so we may well not appreciate the glories of late maturity! So let's together embrace the necessary losses of ageing, the realities of the human condition, and start searching for the soaring beauty that is serenity.

A MEDITATION

Let us begin by centring ourselves: learning to create a space ready to reflect on the business of being human, the business of ageing.

- Choose a time when you have at least a quarter of an hour to spare. Find a quiet place, as free from interruption and disruption as possible. Sit in a comfortable chair with your spine upright, your feet firmly on the floor, and your arms relaxed by your side. Close your eyes.

- Feel the tension in your feet and ankles, and let that tension go. Let your muscles relax, and feel the tension flow out from your feet and ankles to the earth. Now focus on your legs and do the same thing: feel the tension in your muscles and let it go. Now do the same thing with your hips, your spine, your chest, your arms and hands, your neck. Feel the tension around your jaw, your eyes; let it go and relax.

- Notice your breathing. Don't try to change it. Just listen to the rhythms of your body as you relax.

- Notice the sounds that come from outside and inside the room. And then go back to paying attention to your breathing.

- Sit quietly like this for a while. What is passing through your mind? Maybe there is nothing there except stillness. Or maybe you have some thought or image, or some emotion. Notice what it is and accept it; let it pass.

- How do you feel? What does it feel like, to be *still*, in a human body, a human life?

- Accept and acknowledge all your feelings and thoughts.

- Bring your attention back to your breathing and relax.

- And then gradually return to the world.

This technique for deep relaxation may be familiar to you. It is a practice common to many religions, and many non-religious approaches to spirituality too. It should leave you feeling very calm and very aware of yourself at many different levels: body, mind and spirit. This is an excellent place from which to start our exploration of spiritual development in later life. It is also one of the oldest forms of prayer: the oldest form of Christian prayer. Let us call it our "centring" prayer.

THE INVITATION OF CHRIST

Stay with us in meditative calm and listen to the word of God:

Serenity is the gift of God. It is nothing less than a gift wrapped in his love. In giving us the gifts of peace and love God gives us the gift of himself.

God says, "I have loved you with an everlasting love" (Jeremiah 31:3). Totally reliable, unchanging love! Our response to God's love brings an extraordinary gift into our hearts. Jesus says, "Those who love me will keep my word, and my Father will love them, and we will come to them and make our home with them" (John 14:23).

God is at home with us. We don't have to travel a long journey to come into God's presence. We simply have to enter into our own inner being, our heart, and be alone in peace and love with God. St Paul said to the people of Athens, "God… is not far from each one of us. For 'In him we live and move and have our being'" (Acts 17:27-28). At this very moment God is not far from you. God is within you, and a simple movement of your heart in love, in prayer, will bring you into his presence. God wants you to live confidently in his presence with the fullness of his gift of peace.

Christ says, "I came that they may have life, and have it abundantly" (John 10:10). When we find ourselves struggling along the road of life, falling and slipping, losing direction and confused about life and love, Christ says, "Come to me, all you that are weary and are carrying heavy burdens, and I will give you rest. Take my yoke upon you, and learn from me; for I am gentle and humble in heart, and you will find rest for your souls. For my yoke is easy, and my burden is light" (Matthew 11:28-30).

Christ offers us the great gift of inner peace and love. His constant invitation to us is to come to him for rest. Christ doesn't give us false hope. He doesn't promise us a trouble-free life. But he wants to give us peace. He says, "Peace I leave with you; my peace I give to you. I do not give to you as the world gives. Do not let your hearts be troubled, and do not let them be afraid" (John 14:27). This peace survives all travail and loss. It is not an illusory promise of daily bliss without a worry in the world. As the philosopher John Macmurray said:

> The maxim of illusory religion runs: "Fear not; trust in God and He will see that none of the things you fear will happen to you"; that of real religion, on the contrary, is: "Fear not; the things that you are afraid of are quite likely to happen to you, but they are nothing to be afraid of."[5]

The last words Jesus spoke to his disciples in Matthew's Gospel were, "I am with you always, to the end of the age" (Matthew 28:20). Jesus doesn't stand outside our life, aloof from our troubles, fears, sickness and loneliness. He is with us in all our sorrows and joys. In the midst of our suffering, whatever its nature, he gives us this great promise, "your pain will turn into joy" (John 16:20).

The serenity that our heart longs for comes to us as we welcome the presence of Christ into our lives. As we wake up each morning, we wake not just to a new day, but to a fresh realisation of Christ's presence with us. We wake to a new experience of God's love – a love which gives meaning and purpose to the day, even when all kinds of things may be going wrong. This is how St Paul prayed: "…that Christ may dwell in your hearts through faith, as you are being rooted and grounded in love" (Ephesians 3:17). As we wake up each morning to the awareness of God's gift of love in our life, let's offer each new day to him in gratitude for the gift of life. Let's open our hearts to receive God's gift of serenity and inner peace.

Notes

1   L. Trotsky, *Diary in Exile*, 1935 (translation: Atheneum, 1963).

2   Julian of Norwich, *Revelations of Divine Love* (Penguin classics 2003).

3   J. G. Whittier, "Dear Lord and Father of Mankind".

4   R. Peck, "Psychological Developments in the Second Half of Life", B. L. Neugarten (ed.), *Middle Age and Aging: A Reader in Social Psychology* (Chicago: University of Chicago Press, 1968), 88-92. Also: J. M. Stillion and E. E. McDowell, *Suicide Across the Life Span* (London: Routledge, 1996). Also: J. Viorst, *Necessary Losses* (New York: Fawcett, 1986).

5   Quoted in W. A. Barry, *Paying Attention to God* (Notre Dame, IN: Notre Dame Press, 1990), 29.

2

Coming home to our human bodies

"I praise you, for I am fearfully and wonderfully made."
Psalm 139:14

Who is that old person in my mirror? Where did my strength and vigour go? Which of us, in later life, hasn't asked such questions? And which of us, in our secret heart, doesn't carry a label that reads "my real body" – the body I could have, should have – the perfect body, the impossible body, next to which my actual embodied reality is seriously flawed: misshapen in youth, decaying in age?

We human beings have real problems with our bodies. They don't start with ageing, though ageing often brings serious issues to a head: we don't want to be grey and wrinkled; we don't want to need spectacles, a Zimmer frame, hearing aid, or special gadgets to open tins – and worse! But in truth most of us have despaired of our bodies long before we ever begin to age, regretting their style or shape or size, regretting their weakness and frailty… even young people diet, work out, groom, disguise – even the young want more. And beyond these material dissatisfactions is something more profound: the puzzle of how a biological being, an *embodied* being, can live a spiritual life, or find meaning.

Accepting our human embodiment

Ask many a person in the street what religion has to say about the human body, and you're likely to be told that religion views the body as an evil, a distraction, an obstacle to be overcome on the journey to spiritual fulfilment. And one can see where this view comes from. The body is the source of powerful desires, powerful appetites and a variety of lusts, ranging from the sensuality of sex to the lasciviousness of greed, the longing for power or praise, the yearning for safety and security at all costs. Our embodied self can be seen as the source of vanity, jealousy, anger, sinful pride, venal self-interest and self-protective cowardice. And all of this seems to obstruct our journey to the virtue, selfless compassion and contemplative peace that are at the core of spirituality!

Moreover, the body is corrupt, not simply in its power to distract us from virtue, but in its transience. Our human embodiment is only temporary. The physical glories of the body are but a brief summer, followed by a darker autumn, perhaps a bitter winter. How trivial, how meaningless it seems, to be defined by the lusts of such an ephemeral body!

From the beginning of history, human beings have yearned for something that transcends the corruptions of the body: a way of being that lifts us beyond our physical nature to live a life shaped by, and shot through with, the sacred, the eternal – in sum, a life defined by spirituality. Surely, to achieve true spirituality, we must somehow overcome, transcend our bodies. This common idea has been endorsed throughout history by many religious writers from different traditions. In the popular mind, religion, and perhaps especially Christianity, is associated with a rejection of the body and a denial of its goodness and value. Pope Benedict XVI drew attention to this issue in his beautiful encyclical letter, *God Is Love*. He wrote:

> Nowadays Christianity of the past is often criticized as having been opposed to the body: and it is quite true that tendencies of this sort have always existed.[1]

In this negative conception, believers are expected to achieve spirituality by literally repudiating their human embodiment: "mortifying" their bodies by denying themselves the pleasures of the flesh, whether sex or love, comfort, warmth, food or safety – and punishing their bodies for being tempted by these pleasures. In this conception, the body and the pleasures of the flesh – even the pleasures of high self-regard and self-nurture – are enemies of the spirit and must be put aside if we are to find spiritual fulfilment.

But for Catholics, this popular conception of religion is a *misconception*. In fact, it's an ancient heresy: the heresy of Manicheism, which arose in the third century AD and still influences us today. Like the Greek philosopher Plato, the Persian philosopher Mani (who founded Manicheism) believed that body and spirit are at war with each other, and that the spirit is imprisoned in the body. The body is evil and to be rejected so that the spirit may be freed. Pope John Paul II states, in his wonderful *Theology of the Body*, that this is a very mistaken idea: "The Manichean way of understanding and evaluating the human body and sexuality is essentially foreign to the Gospel."[2]

We are "body-persons" and our spiritual development will always depend on our embodiment. The human body, far from being a prison for the spirit, is "...a sign of the person, a manifestation of the spirit".[3] Indeed John Paul says that "Man expresses himself by means of the body, and in this sense, I would say 'is' that body."[4] In other words, we don't just *have* a body, we *are* our body.[5]

From this point of view, what is done to our body is done to our person. In rejecting, neglecting or abusing the body, as Manicheism demands, John Paul points out that we do ourselves profound damage, for we turn away from and refuse to engage with natural human life and development, or the real challenges of the human condition – and in so doing, we turn away from the very experiences which might shape our true spirituality!

Instead of viewing the body as a hindrance to spirituality, Pope John Paul argues for a specific "spirituality of the body".[6] For the body is not the enemy of spirituality: quite the reverse! In fact, it is only through embracing the realities of our human condition and the direct experience of our own personal human journey that we face the challenges which invite us to develop as spiritual beings. John Paul explains that there can be no spirituality without our humanity: without our "corrupt" bodies we would have no need to develop the resources of courage and compassion, of virtue, faith and serenity, which we call spiritual. Our spirituality may be the flower of our existence, the fulfilment of our human development, but that flower cannot blossom without its roots in the fertile soil of our humanity. Our spirituality grows through our humanity, and withers as we reject that humanity.

From this perspective, living a spiritual life is not a matter of rejecting or denying our human embodiment, but of *embracing* it and learning all that we can through the revelation offered by our human journey. We believe that our human lives and experiences constantly invite us to discover new insights, new strengths, new understanding, and through this to develop a new maturity rich in spiritual power. These insights are not always what we expect or want! But that is the nature of insight, whether in science, faith or everyday life.

Do we make the most of the invitations which are an intrinsic part of our human condition? Too often we don't. We are ill at ease, uncomfortable, even at war with a body that seems imperfect and unsatisfactory. Accepting the insights offered by the human condition seems too hard. We excuse our spiritual failures by calling ourselves "*only* human", as if that were something inherently inadequate, to be apologised for. Rather than rejoicing in our humanity for what it is and reaching for the gifts it offers, we simply wish we weren't starting from here.

The joyful message of John Paul's teaching is that it's not just *okay* to be human, but *glorious*! Our whole embodied being has been redeemed. There is no need to feel inadequate or to apologise for our humanity, not even to ourselves. The very things which disturb us – from our mortality to our tendency to think and do things we regret – are the very things we should rejoice in, because they are the very things which shape our journey towards a spiritual destination! Without the "corruptions" of the human condition there is nothing to react to, nothing to motivate us towards the moral values or the contemplative experience of serenity, of connection with creation – with God – that we so revere! "Sweet is the rose, but grows upon a briar."[7] Without the briar it would not be a rose. We are what we are – creatures capable of a sublime morality and transcendental serenity, precisely *because* we are human, with all that entails. Not despite that fact!

Here is a first foundation for serenity: coming home to our basic human condition, believing our humanity is a glorious home to be treasured and lived in as richly as possible, *just as it is*. Not wishing we were some other kind of creature, or starting from somewhere else. This joyful acceptance of the human condition is vital to serenity at any time of life – but especially in old age.

Accepting our own bodies

If the first step in our journey to serenity is coming home to and embracing our essential humanity, the second is coming home to the particular human being, the particular human body that is *me*. And if we have problems coming to see embodiment as a gift rather than an obstacle to spiritual development, that is as nothing compared to the problems we have in coming to terms with our individual bodies!

Most of us – even celebrities or skilled athletes – wish that our faces or bodies looked – or behaved – differently from how they actually do. In the newspaper at the time of writing, for instance, there is a story about a famous and handsome actor, who wishes his face were more aristocratic; a woman who describes her desperate but futile efforts to change her natural body shape; another whose epic (and unsuccessful) struggle to lose weight dominates her life; a woman whose eating disorder has destroyed her ability to bear children; a young man whose quest for strength led him to take dangerous steroids; a woman so dissatisfied with her appearance that she went for plastic surgery – which first crippled, then, over a few years, killed her.

Dissatisfaction with our bodies is almost universal, even among the beautiful and the athletic. It creeps in very early, even in childhood, as we become aware of how we appear in relation to other people, or to some theoretical ideal. It escalates through adolescence, and for most people never really fades. Only the happy few have never disliked some aspect of their own body – either looks or strength or stamina! Astonishing amounts of the earth's resources, time, effort, misery and money are put into trying to disguise or remedy what are widely considered to be bodily defects – even among the attractive, healthy and young!

But *why* are we so unhappy with our bodies? And what has this to do with spirituality or serenity? Ask a plastic surgeon or psychologist and you'll find that very often our dissatisfaction with our appearance masks a deeper dissatisfaction with our selves: a rejection at the very core of self, which has somehow become attached to some peripheral part of the body (a nose, an ear, breasts or pectoral muscles that are somehow the wrong shape or size). We seem to believe that, if only the offending part of the body could be fixed, the dissatisfaction with *myself* and my life would be fixed, too. Sadly (but unsurprisingly) this hardly ever turns out to be true. The reality is that I can only fix dissatisfaction with myself as a whole by addressing my whole self, not some peripheral part. The problem is not material but spiritual. As John Paul loved to say, the body manifests the person. If I am at peace within myself I am surely at peace with my body.

Of course, our bodies matter enormously in shaping who we are. Key aspects of our bodies, such as gender, skin colour, disposition to be fat or thin, beautiful or plain, healthy or otherwise, temperamental or placid, quick-witted or slow, have an enormous impact on how people treat us, what they expect of us, and what opportunities we have in life. And these things have an enormous impact on what we learn and how we develop – on the people we become. Born as a different body, my life would have been very different – and there is no denying that!

But the notion that our bodies shape our destinies is only partly right. Yes: born beautiful and strong we may be given many opportunities denied to the weak or plain. Yes: born with a disability in a society which marginalises disabled people, or born female in a society which gives girls no education, no rights, no freedom of choice, an individual may have very limited material possibilities. But no circumstance can determine how the individual reacts to such opportunities or limitations. We all have choices. For example, someone blessed with breathtaking beauty might focus narcissistically on his or her appearance, rather than developing fully as a human being. Equally, a plain person might become bitter, or find values that are more lasting. Many a man in pre-modern England, despite the freedoms and privileges which were denied to women of the day, achieved far less than the novelist Jane Austen, the nurse Florence Nightingale or the social reformer Elizabeth Fry! Nelson Mandela and Aung Sang Suu Kyi have done more for the fight for justice, from behind prison bars, than virtually any of us who live in freedom. Few of us can imagine coping with life confined to a wheelchair, even dependent on a machine to breathe – indeed, many might consider it a life not worth living. Yet there is the example of Jane Campbell, who was predicted to die in infancy and, more recently, underwent the indignity of doctors putting a "do not resuscitate" notice on her medical records. Yet she has spent much of her life campaigning for society to see people with disabilities as simply human beings like any other, earning a life peerage in the process. Now over 50, Jane Campbell, Baroness Campbell of Surbiton, is still going strong! Or take Professor Stephen Hawking, whose computer-generated voice is familiar to millions. Despite his disabilities, he has made astonishing contributions to theoretical physics. Or guardsman Simon Weston, whose face was appallingly burned in the Falklands War, but who has drawn on his strength of character to help so many people. Or... you can think of many more to add to this list, not just the famous, but the unsung everyday heroes and heroines who transcend difficulties.

The human spirit can sink despite all the advantages of life, and a depressing number of gifted, beautiful, strong and privileged people do exactly that – as is clear from endless news stories about footballers, pop stars, politicians and the rich and famous. But the human spirit can also soar, even above severe limitations, and that's true not just for exceptional individuals, but for everyone who copes courageously and wisely with adversity, illness or infirmity, disfigurement or disease. It's not the circumstances our bodies create, but the *attitudes* and *values* we develop, which determine whether we sink or soar. In other words, it is our *spiritual response*, not the material situation, which ultimately determines who and how we are.

The truth is that our dissatisfaction with our bodies reflects a spiritual malaise, a discomfort, an uneasiness in the life that *this* body is living. We are not at home with who we are, and wish we were living differently. We see how aspects of our bodies have shaped our lives, and focus on wishing those things were different. We imagine that fixing them will put us right, rather than realising we can only heal by developing and exploring the spiritual potential that will bring real peace.

What stops so many people from developing their full human and spiritual potential? It's certainly true that some lives seem to offer much better opportunities than others. We need, in solidarity, to work for all to have a more equal start, a more equal chance. But soaring spirituality isn't guaranteed in the fortunate, nor impossible for the less favoured, as we have already seen! It is shamefully absent in too many privileged lives, and it emerges in the most unlikely lives, the most unlikely people. Circumstances don't determine who we are or what we can be. A more crucial factor is self-belief: the assurance to say, *I am as good as any other, whatever my circumstances may be. I am as capable of soaring spirituality. I am as significant, I matter as much as any other.* But how many of us have that healthy kind of self-esteem?

We make so many mistakes over self-esteem. Sometimes we search for value in being superior to others, puffing ourselves up by imagining that we are of more worth than anyone who seems to lack our particular talents or qualities. But such competitiveness breeds only invidious pride. A healthy self-esteem is rooted, not in competition, but in self-acceptance. But so many of us struggle to find that self-acceptance, thinking badly of ourselves! It is the lack of self-acceptance, the lack of healthy self-esteem rooted in love for *my* particular, personal embodiment, which holds us back from reaching our full human potential: *who am I to aspire to such a thing?*

Why do we so doubt, and so undermine ourselves? Too often we judge our personal worth and potential by absurd standards. We compare our beauty, wealth, intelligence and achievements with the most favoured of our species, and find ourselves lacking. Or else we judge ourselves against standards of moral and spiritual perfection, and find ourselves worse than lacking. We start to believe that we are inadequate – that nothing much can spring from such poor soil. We set our material expectations low. And we come to believe that spiritual strength can't be achieved from here: not starting from *me*.

In theory, believer or unbeliever, we are committed to the idea that every human life is as valuable, as significant as any other *no matter what he or she may or may not have achieved*, and that everyone has the right to explore and develop his or her full potential. The idea is enshrined in the entirely secular International Treaty of Human Rights.[8] It is at the heart of many religious traditions, and of our Christian faith, too – we are all, whoever we are, equal in the eyes of God, and all equally and individually called to spiritual development: "I have called you by name, you are mine" (Isaiah 43:1). The trouble is that in practice we don't believe it! We don't believe the promise, the potential which is ours. We don't dare to believe it. We can believe it for others, but, secretly, we don't dare believe that *we ourselves* embody that potential! And so we undermine ourselves with doubts, and set our horizons low. Here is spiritual failure indeed! Here is a failure of self-esteem which robs us of our spiritual potential, our potential for serenity.

Healthy self-esteem does not come from the absurd comparisons we make between ourselves and others, or between ourselves and ideal aspirations. In the shifting sands of our ever-changing world, such material comparisons can give no stable basis for self-worth. Healthy self-esteem comes from accepting our unchanging, universal value: from truly accepting that *every* human being is of equal value, equal worth – and that this includes *me*. Stephanie's father used to express this by saying, "There is no one less capable of finding spiritual strength than me, and no one more capable of finding it either." Here is healthy humility – *no one less...* – and healthy self-esteem: *no one more*. Here is the basis of true self-esteem, built on spiritual values, not material comparisons! Here is self-esteem that lets us feel joy and thankfulness in our own bodies and lives, whatever they may be. Here is self-esteem that sets us free to fully explore our spiritual potential. Here is the self-esteem we should strive for through all our lives, as much in youth as in age, but which eludes too many, even in later life.

Here is the second foundation for serenity: coming home to our own individual embodiment, to be comfortable, happy and at peace with whatever particular human life we may be living. The challenge is to love myself as I am: to develop a self-esteem which truly allows me to feel that it's okay to be *me* and that I am as valuable, and as capable of developing and finding spiritual fulfilment, as anyone!

Accepting the ageing body

Whatever age we are, it's hard to accept that our human condition is a gift rather than an obstacle to spiritual development, and it's hard to embrace the kind of self-esteem which frees us to search for that development for ourselves. In youth we are often distracted from these challenges by the hurly-burly of everyday life. Or else we put things off until later, with the result that most of us reach later life without having built either of the first two foundations of serenity. But as we age, both issues come to the fore. The questions of how to find meaning, virtue and serenity in this life – and in *my* life – become more urgent but, sadly, no easier.

Our society is obsessed by age. Or, to be exact, we are obsessed by youth. Our television schedules are crammed with programmes advising us on how to look "ten years younger", or how to change our lifestyle so as to feel ten years younger, or live ten years longer. It's as if the only acceptable way to be is young. Over a certain age we are regarded – and regard ourselves – as being past our "sell-by date", over the hill. We too often feel, as one friend (a healthy, good-looking 70-year-old) recently put it, "My life is over." Yet it wasn't always so. Speaking in 1971, the fashion designer Coco Chanel commented: "Youth is something very new: twenty years ago no one mentioned it."[9] And in other cultures, youth is not revered as it is with us. Other cultures place greater value on the wisdom of experience, rather than the smooth face of youth which so obsesses us. In other cultures, the silver hair and wrinkles which cause us such despair are marks of achievement, earning respect!

Why are we so obsessed with youth? Why is it not okay to be old? Why, for so very many, is the advent of ageing so very depressing? Of course, there are aspects of ageing which it is natural to fear, such as illness, infirmity, the loss of the strength and vigour of the mind and body on which we have so long relied. Even in cultures which revere the wisdom of age, these things are difficult to come to terms with. In certain ways, as the poet Juvenal put it almost 2,000 years ago, "ageing is more to be feared than death".[10] But it is remarkable to think that we – who live in a society where medicine and science are better able to cope with these problems than ever before, who are stronger and healthier in our later years than any other generation – *we* are the most afraid of ageing! *We* strive the hardest to avoid the signs, the appearance (the realities) of ageing.

What is there to fear in looking older, if we still have our health, as many do? Is it as misguidedly shallow as the fear that one must, as the song puts it, "keep young and beautiful if you want to be loved"? Our society is as obsessed with sex as with youth, and with the youthful looks that are considered "sexy". As youthful looks pass and our faces and bodies begin to reflect the decades and signs of illness or injury, many people would echo the woman who said, "no one could love me, looking like this". But the fact is that beauty is neither sufficient nor necessary for love: in fact, it's often a monumental distraction. Many of the world's most beautiful women have suffered miserable personal lives devoid of real love, because few people have looked beyond their physical beauty, or seen them as a whole person. But a trip around any supermarket or hospital reveals many an unprepossessing individual hand in hand with a long-lasting love. The truth is that love is not really about sex or beauty, it's about the *gift of self* – the profound, intimate and caring connection between one person and another; the mutuality that shares all the ups and downs of experience. And that gift of self is open to us *all*, to give and receive, whatever we look like and whatever our age. What sane person could possibly prefer to be sought out for their slim hips, their beautiful legs or unlined face, rather than for the generosity of their heart or the life-enhancing joy of their presence?

Are we driven to look young in order to avoid seeming like yesterday's people in tomorrow's world? Our society is as obsessed with progress, with novelty and change, as with sex. We want new young faces at the helm in politics, the arts and science. It's as though we believe that youth, of itself, carries with it the qualities of creativity and originality, while age automatically means doing things the old way and stagnating! And yet many of the greatest achievements of our culture are the achievements of maturity. Most breakthroughs in science and medicine, technology and the arts, and spirituality, are the fruits of long training and experience, rather than the spontaneous creativity of youth – so much so that the occasional youthful contributors are singled out as prodigies! And many of the greatest achievements of our species, material or spiritual, are the product not only of mature individual experience, but of wisdom built up across generations: wisdom rooted in the old ways.

There are doubtless many things which make us fear the appearance of ageing. But at the core of this fear is a spiritual emptiness which means we cannot bear the physical signs of ageing because of what they symbolise. We cannot bear to be reminded that the adult body, the adult life we know, is transient and will come to an end. We look at the signs of ageing with a secret combination of pity and dread, seeing in the ruined faces, of the very old, or in the first withering of our own faces, a challenge that we are not ready to take. Somehow, the giant strides of science and medicine have convinced us that we might, one day, avoid that challenge: that we might be able to stop the ageing process altogether, not only remaining youthful and healthy for a long time, but even maybe living this life for ever. To be reminded that this is not so frightens us. But in committing ourselves to hope for such an immortal humanity, we are turning away from some of the human spirit's greatest challenges. Technology and science have not, in reality, rescued us from those challenges, and are not likely to. We will still have to face them. But with our faith in technology, we have lost the art of spiritual exploration in this area.

Viewed from Mars, as it were, it might look very much as if society is in a state of arrested development. Why are we so concerned to preserve for ever the middle part of our life cycle? Why so reluctant to pass on to the next stage? Nature is full of changes and transitions – the spawn gives way to the tadpole, the tadpole to the frog – and who is to say which is the more beautiful? Certainly the middle phase of a life cycle is not necessarily the most attractive: the caterpillar enters the dark chrysalis and only emerges in full glory as a butterfly at the end of its life. Every stage of life may have its own glories, its own purpose. A rosebud is beautiful, but must give way to the very different beauty of the flower – and the rose is beautiful, but must give way to the very different beauty of the rosehip if the cycle of life is to come to fruition. We, too, are biological beings with a natural life cycle. But rather than embracing the purposes and possibilities of each stage of life, we fight to stay in the middle of our lives, as if achieving full maturity were an enemy to be fought off at all costs!

As we contemplate the ageing of the body, we are confronted afresh with the spiritual challenges of being human, of being *me*, and all too often we do so without the foundations we need to engage with this stage of life with serenity. The "corruptions" of our human embodiment come into clearer focus, and rather than appreciating them as the springboard from which our spirituality can soar into serenity and fulfilment, we want to run away. Lacking a healthy self-esteem, we imagine our worth seeping even further away as our looks and strength fade, and our satisfaction with our own lives, which is often weak, crumbles. It is not too late to mend all this; not too late to build the first two foundations of serenity! In fact, now is the time.

And as for the special challenges of the ageing body? The key is to accept that life has a cycle, and that each stage has its own purpose. A healthy self-esteem has nothing to do with looks or strength, nothing to do with our achievements or lack of achievements, and is not affected by ageing. The later years of life have their own special spiritual possibilities, which we shall explore through successive chapters in this book – possibilities we can only realise by letting go of youth and engaging with that later part of our human journey. We need not rush to "look the part" – we need not, indeed should not, stop nurturing our bodies and making the best of them! But we should shift our perspective. The withering of the rose may seem like decay from the flower's perspective, but marks only the start of fulfilment for the rosehip, and for the fruition of the plant as a whole.

The third foundation of serenity is to throw away the idea that ageing is the decaying of life. It is merely the passing of the flower of youth, giving way to the full fruit of maturity. The third foundation of serenity is to come home, joyfully, to the potential, the gifts of life inherent in our fruition, in fulfilling the human life cycle.

A MEDITATION

Let us begin by centring ourselves: creating a space ready to reflect.

- Choose a time when you have at least a quarter of an hour to spare. Find a quiet place, as free from interruption and disruption as possible. Sit in a comfortable chair with your spine upright, your feet firmly on the floor, and your arms relaxed by your side. Close your eyes.

- Feel the tension in your feet and ankles, and let that tension go. Let your muscles relax, and feel the tension flow out from your feet and ankles to the earth. Now focus on your legs and do the same thing: feel the tension in your muscles and let it go. Now do the same thing with your hips, your spine, your chest, your arms and hands, your neck. Feel the tension around your jaw, your eyes; let it go and relax.

- Notice your breathing. Don't try to change it. Just listen to the rhythms of your body as you relax.

- Notice the sounds that come from outside and inside the room. And then go back to paying attention to your breathing.

- Sit quietly like this for a while. What is passing through your mind? Maybe there is nothing there except stillness. Or maybe you have some thought or image, or some emotion. Notice what it is and accept it; let it pass.

- How does it feel to be *human*, with all the shared peculiarities, paradoxes, glories and terrors of this embodied state? Can you believe that this human condition is not an obstacle, but a gateway to spirituality and serenity?

- How does it feel to be uniquely *you*, manifest in a particular body, a particular situation? Can you truly believe that there is no one less able, but no one more able than you to find spiritual fulfilment?

- How does it feel to be *ageing*? Are you ready to engage the rich spiritual possibilities of later life, the fruition of human life?

- Accept and acknowledge all your feelings and thoughts.

- Bring your attention back to your breathing and relax.

- And then gradually return to the world.

We worry ourselves ragged over the issues of our humanity, the physical and moral frailty of our human condition; over the question of *myself,* and what I do or ever could amount to. We cling to the flower of our youth, seeing only decay as it fades. How liberating, how joyful would it be if we could embrace human frailty as a spiritual gift, find ultimate value in ourselves, and accept with gratitude the grace of completing a human life! Believer or unbeliever, here is the spiritual invitation of later life. Here is the invitation to serenity. And, for believers, here is the invitation to reach out for the peace of God: the peace which surpasses all understanding.

THE INVITATION OF CHRIST

Stay with us in meditative calm and listen to the word of God:

The Bible tells us that God created us "...in his image, in the image of God" (Genesis 1:27). Our whole being has been made in the image of God! And this is as true in age as in youth.

Commenting on the phrase "the Word became flesh" (John 1:14), St Athanasius wrote in the fourth century:

> The human body has been greatly enhanced through fellowship and union of the Word with it. From being mortal, it has become immortal; though physical, it has become spiritual; though made of earth, it has passed through the gates of heaven.[11]

In the great mystery of our faith, the mystery of God becoming man, one like us, we see the profound depth of what it means to be an embodied person. Jesus Christ, truly God and truly a human being, has united our human nature to the divine nature and, in doing so, has for ever transformed human nature. Our bodies, St Paul can tell us, are the temple of the Holy Spirit. This is what he wrote to the first Christian community in Corinth:

> Do you not know that your body is a temple of the Holy Spirit within you, which you have from God, and that you are not your own? For you were bought with a price; therefore glorify God in your body. (1 Corinthians 6:19-20)

Everything we do, every good work, every act of kindness, we do through our bodies. When you come to worship God it is through your body that you offer your gifts. When you kneel or stand or sit to pray, it is through your body that your heart seeks communion with God. It is through your body that you show loving kindness to another person. In fact, everything that is good and holy and hopeful in our lives becomes manifest through our bodies. This is why Pope John Paul can say:

> The body, and it alone, is capable of making visible what is invisible: the spiritual and divine. It was created to transfer into the visible reality of the world, the mystery hidden since time immemorial in God, and thus to be a sign of it.[12]

Made in God's image and likeness, there is nothing in the whole of creation more like God than the embodied person. Why? Because the image of God in our bodies is inscribed in our capacity to love others as God loves us. It is in and through our body, weak and sinful though we may be, that we love with God's love. God is love and you, as the image of God, have the capacity to love as God loves. The image of God in your body enables you to reflect God's love through your body.

We can say, in very Catholic language, that your body is the sacrament of yourself, the visible manifestation of your person.

And it is your person, made visible and tangible to others through your body, who loves as God loves. Without your body you would have no presence to others; without your body, you would not have the capacity to love as God loves. Pope John Paul called this capacity to love "the spousal meaning of the body". This is how he defined it:

> The spousal meaning of the body includes from the beginning the spousal attribute, that is, the capacity of expressing love, that love in which the person becomes a gift and – by means of this gift – fulfils the meaning of his being and existence.[13]

God makes a gift of himself to us and we, being in God's image, can make a gift of self to others. That is the dignity of our body. The Holy Spirit inspires this beautiful prayer:

> For it was you who formed my inward parts; you knit me together in my mother's womb. I praise you, for I am fearfully and wonderfully made. Wonderful are your works; that I know very well. (Psalm 139:13-14)

Your body is a wonder because it radiates the glory of God. And none of the glory of our human embodiment dims with age. We remain in God's image, and indeed, we can grow daily into his likeness as we mature in loving as God loves us.

Notes

1   Benedict XVI, *Deus Caritas Est* [God is love], 5.

2   *Man and Woman He Created Them: A Theology of the Body*, trans. Michael Waldstein (Boston: Pauline Books & Media, 2006), 55.4. John Paul worked on *Theology of the Body* through the first five years of his time as pope, through a series of 129 talks collected in this book. His biographer George Weigel asserts that "If it is taken with the seriousness it deserves, John Paul's *Theology of the Body* may prove the decisive moment in exorcising the Manichean demon and its depreciation of human sexuality from Catholic moral theology" (G. Weigel, *Witness to Hope* [London: HarperCollins, 1999], 342).

3   John Paul II, *Man and Woman He Created Them*, 59.3.

4   As above, 55.2.

5   *Catechism of the Catholic Church* (365) makes a clear statement on this: "The unity of soul and body is so profound that one has to consider the soul to be the 'form' of the body: i.e., it is because of its spiritual soul that the body made of matter becomes a living, human body; spirit and matter, in humans, are not two natures united, but rather, their union forms a single nature."

6   John Paul II, *Man and Woman He Created Them*, 59.4.

7   Edmund Spenser, *Amoretti* Sonnet 26 (London: Ponsonby, 1595).

8   There are a number of treaties collectively referred to as the "International bill of human rights" but popularly referred to as the "international treaty of human rights". The core of these is the Universal Declaration of Human Rights, ratified at the United Nations General Assembly on 10 December 1948 at the Palais de Chaillot in Paris.

9   Quoted in M. Haedrich, *Coco Chanel: Her Life, Her Secrets* (London: Little, Brown, 1979).

10   Quoted in E. Katz, *Old Age Comes at a Bad Time* (London: Robson Books, 1997), 43.

11   Office of Readings, 1 January.

12   John Paul II, *Man and Woman He Created Them*, 19.4.

13   As above, 15.1.

3

Embracing a personal identity

"Who am I, O Lord God... that you have brought me thus far?"
2 Samuel 7:18

If the first spiritual challenge of later life is coming home to our human bodies, the second is discovering and embracing a real personal identity.

Through most of our lives, our identities are intimately bound up in and defined by the work we do. Asked to describe ourselves, we usually present an identity bound up with what we do: *I am a housewife, a mother, a priest, a plumber, a health visitor, a doctor, an actor, an electrician...* But at some point in later life, the children we have nurtured become adult and leave home, and our careers wind down towards retirement. The identity defined by our occupation comes to an end. And for many, this presents a real crisis. As one woman put it, on reaching retirement: "I used to be a head teacher; but who am I now?"[1]

Coming to terms with retirement

The "baby boomers" coming up to retirement now are the first (and will very likely be the last) generation to retire while they are still strong in mind and body, to live decades of healthy, vigorous life on comfortable pensions. The vast majority of our predecessors left their work only a few years before they died – already old and tired. The vast majority of our descendants will not have the luxury of long retirement – as the pensions crisis deepens they too will be likely to have to work almost until the end. Those of us who have long retirements are privileged indeed! But retirement doesn't always feel like a privilege.

For some, retirement is a release from the drudgery of an unsatisfactory career. It offers the prospect of the endless holiday they have always longed for, dreamed of, planned for. They look forward eagerly to retiring, and take their leave from work as early as they can. And for some of these, the dream comes true: life changes for the better and becomes more fulfilling. They find a new identity in their leisure activities. But for many, living the dream turns out to be a disappointment. Sometimes, it is the material world which disappoints: the grass turns out not to be greener somewhere else. But often, the disappointment is more subtle. What had made holidays enchanting in the past was their rarity: the few weeks outside of normal routine, the novelty, the chance to explore new places, new activities, to relax. For many of us, it is hard to be as excited by a glorious view (say) that you see every day as you were the first few times you saw it; and it is not so much fun being "busy doing nothing" month after month, year after year, as it is to take one's ease on a short holiday. Gradually, an emptiness can creep into life.

For some, the prospect of retirement is, and always has been, more threat than reward. For those who can imagine no other life, or those who love their work, particularly if that work involves important responsibilities – such as caring for young people or being involved in physical, medical, intellectual or spiritual wellbeing – retirement seems to take away life's purpose and meaning. The very prospect of retirement holds a sense of emptiness – a loss of direction and identity: *who am I, what shall I do now?* Often, for people in this situation, retirement brings grief – a feeling of no longer being needed, or making a contribution, or being part of the enterprises, great or small, to which they have given their adult lives. Retirement brings feelings, not so much of release from a chore, as of uselessness and helplessness; not so much of freedom, as of disconnection – as though life had been shunted into some sideline with no future prospect. The poet Robert Frost captured the essence of this pain in his poem "Provide, Provide":

> No memory of having starred
> Atones for later disregard
> Or keeps the end from being hard.[2]

What are we supposed to do with our time and talents in retirement? For those who are happy to holiday forever there is no problem. But for others this is a real challenge. For most of our lives our work has structured our days. As we lay down our responsibilities, we lose that structure. Many in early retirement find themselves getting up later and later in the day, doing less and less. Some become depressed; time drags through the empty days. Most people pull themselves together after a while, establishing new routines around social activities or voluntary work. We fill our time so effectively that, quite soon, we wonder how we ever had time to go to work!

Keeping active in retirement is a healthy strategy. Scientists tell us that the more we exercise our bodies, the more we use our brains, the more we socialise, the longer we are likely to stay strong and alert. The saying "use it or lose it" is absolutely right! Taking up golf or bridge, for example, using old skills to help others, learning a new skill or language, walking every day – all such activities keep our bodies and minds in good order. Some say that the very best thing is to take up Scottish country dancing, which combines physical exercise with mental exercise, in mastering the intricacies of the steps, and social contact and touch – the perfect combination of the things we need to stay physically and emotionally healthy!

For many, re-establishing routines and an active life in retirement in this way is fulfilling. And using our talents and nurturing our bodies is not only a physically healthy approach to retirement – it's spiritually healthy too: coming home to our bodies is as much a matter of looking after them and using them as it is of loving and accepting them. But is this *all*, is this the whole spiritual challenge of later life? Do we just dance our days away?

The French use the same word – *retraite* – to mean both retirement and spiritual retreat. In other cultures, too, there is a strong association between putting down the responsibilities of work and actively engaging in a more spiritual journey. Some Hindus put down not only their responsibilities, but all their possessions and the patterns of their lives, to wander as holy beggars, devoting their time to this spiritual search. For all of us, whether or not our language or culture makes the connection so explicitly, retirement raises questions about the meaning and purpose of life: spiritual questions.

The journey into spiritual fulfilment in later life is complex and multi-faceted, led by many different things, as we shall explore through the successive chapters of this book. But what, specifically, is the spiritual challenge associated with laying down our working lives?

Who am I, Lord? If I am no longer doctor, lawyer, teacher, who am I? The core spiritual challenge posed by retirement is to find a new identity – and not just by swapping one material identity, one label, for another. Rather, the challenge is to find an identity which transcends the work we do or the activities in which we engage. I may play bridge, dance, teach, publish research, but I am much more than a bridge-player, a dancer, a teacher, a writer. The challenge of later life is to explore who I truly am beneath those labels.

Of course, we have always been much more than the roles we've worked in, as important (and often constructive) as those roles have been. But often, they have dominated our lives, shaping our identities and experience, shaping how others react to us. Often in our busy lives, they have also dominated our own sense of self. Take the role away, and we scarcely know who we are. The psychiatrist Bruno Bettelheim, who survived a period in the Nazi concentration camps of Dachau and Buchenwald, observed that people whose identities are bound up in the roles they play may struggle to survive mentally when those roles are abruptly taken away.[3] It is those whose identities transcend their roles who have the inner strength to survive and stay true to themselves, no matter what may come their way.

More systematic study[4] of individuals who have shown immense inner strength in difficult circumstances confirms that their identity is rooted in *values* rather than work-defined roles. Such individuals have a clearer and more elaborated understanding of their core values than others – values which always include compassion, courage, justice and integrity. Where others are focused on fulfilling the demands of a particular role, these individuals are focused on trying to live up to their core values. They do not believe that they actually manage this all the time – far from it! They have a frank and honest assessment of themselves. But where others might view such a gap between aspiration and reality with despair, they view it with an engaging hope, seeing themselves as "works in progress", ever striving forward. They see themselves as having a personal responsibility for the welfare of others and for the welfare of the world, and they try to discern just what that responsibility is and how to fulfil it. It is this commitment to shaping life around values, around what really matters, which gives these individuals an identity that can withstand almost anything, intact and focused. These are the kind of people who impress us. They are the stuff of which saints are made.

Some individuals develop an identity powerfully rooted in values rather than roles early in life: one thinks of the young men and women over the centuries who have committed themselves to a moral cause or vocation, perhaps even risking their lives for it. But this is rare. Caught up in our busy everyday lives, caught up in the demands of our work, most of us don't have the time and space or the opportunity to fully develop an identity at this level until we retire. Of course, we have always had values, and those values have always influenced our lives. But they haven't always been the core, the driving force of our lives as they are for the special few.

Why should we want or need an identity driven by values in later life, especially as our working day is done and responsibility for the world begins to pass to the hands of a new generation? It is never too late to take personal responsibility for the welfare of others, for the peace and justice of our world, even if all one can do is raise a voice or provide a living example. It's never too late to make courage and compassion, justice and integrity the cornerstones of our identity. Science and religion combine to tell us that this is the mature fulfilment of human development. This is the path of conversion Christ calls us to. We are beings innately disposed toward these virtues, with a vast capacity for moral development, that is too seldom fulfilled. We are beings who find immense peace in feeling that we are doing the right thing, that we are virtuous. In sum, we are beings whose human development is fulfilled in the achievement of a spiritual identity rooted in values! This is what we mean by spiritual strength, and achieving it at any age yields the peace and joy, the serenity that comes from knowing that one's life is "in the right place", that one is doing the right thing.

Spiritual strength is a vital resource on our journey through later life. Retirement is only the first stage of ageing: however healthy we may be at first, however happy in our new activities, the path ahead is uncertain. Sooner or later as we approach old age, most of us have to face illness or frailty which will change and constrain our lives forever. We have to face bereavement, as those we love and share our lives with die or fade into dementia. And we have to face up to our own death. As the actress Bette Davis said, "old age is not for sissies". Now, in early retirement, is the time to prepare for that uncertain future, to strengthen the inner resources we shall need to cope with whatever may come our way.

In sum, retirement challenges us to grow from an identity rooted in our work or play into an identity more profoundly rooted in the eternal values of compassion, courage, integrity and justice. Developing this new depth of character is a cornerstone for spiritual fulfilment and serenity in later life.

Coming to know myself

Who am I, Lord? Personal growth is a journey. And, like any journey, we need a map to get from A to B. Like any other journey, it's possible to get lost for many different reasons.

One of the authors, Stephanie, recalls making a car journey many years ago from Brighton to Verona with her dearest friend. Stephanie drove, while her friend read the maps. All went well until the third morning. Wending their way through a maze of streets on the outskirts of a town in France, Stephanie's companion announced that she should turn right, and would find herself on the sliproad to the motorway to Switzerland. In fact, that right turn took them into a cul-de-sac on a housing estate… A short "discussion" about this unexpected denouement revealed that, not quite sure where they were starting from, the navigator had made an intelligent but unfortunately incorrect guess – and directed Stephanie from there!

As in car journeys, so in spiritual journeys, our attention is focused on the destination we hope to reach. But all too often we lay our spiritual plans without really knowing where we are starting from. And, as with car journeys, such confusions can lead to cul-de-sacs rather than the highway we hope for!

How well do you know yourself? What are you really like? Research by leading psychologist David Dunning suggests that most of us have a highly inaccurate picture of ourselves, particularly when it comes to knowing the values that motivate us:[5] we overestimate our virtues – and our vices. We aren't good at predicting how we will behave in various circumstances, or how we will feel. We are very poor, for example, at anticipating what will make us happy, or how we will react in a crisis. We don't see ourselves as others see us! And, by and large, their view is more accurate than our own: their predictions of how we will react in one situation or another are often more accurate than ours.

We all know people whose view of themselves is vastly inaccurate (the famously difficult woman, for example, who once reduced her family to helpless coughing by announcing that she was "not a person to make a fuss"). The secret, as Dunning says, is *to know when the person with poor self-perception is me!*

Why is it so hard to know ourselves? Dunning suggests that there are a number of things which make it objectively very difficult to see ourselves accurately, the chief of which is that we see ourselves (inevitably) from only one perspective: our own. Often, we simply don't have the right information to assess ourselves accurately. Like the three-year-old who proudly boasts that he knows the whole alphabet, "A, B, C, G, K, M, S, T, Y, Z!" we simply don't know what is missing from our knowledge. If I don't know that there is a better way of being a parent, friend, lover (say), or that there is a different, perhaps better way to handle strife or disappointment, or to meet some existential challenge or fear, then I have no basis for judging how well or badly I am doing. If I don't know how other people will react in a given situation, then how can I know whether I am brave or cowardly, impulsive or reflective, decisive or indecisive?

Dunning's recipe for self-knowledge is simple: (1) start noticing how well (or badly) your predictions about how you will behave in a given situation meet the facts, and adjust your self-concept accordingly; (2) "benchmark" – compare how you react to a given situation with how others react, and learn about yourself, and what other ways of being may be possible, from the comparison; (3) ask those who love you to describe your character – and, if several people say the same things, *believe them*!

Lack of information about ourselves is one thing. But in the area of self-knowledge, there is also the problem of unwelcome knowledge. There are things about ourselves which we would rather not know, particularly when it comes to realising how far we do or don't live up to the values we hold! For how can I love and respect myself, if I admit that I can be selfish, or unkind, or dishonest – or worse? Even a half-acknowledged dismay at my own shortcomings is enough to seriously dent my self-esteem.

It takes courage to take a long, hard look at oneself and make an honest appraisal of one's vices and virtues. To be honest about one's vices is hard enough: it's difficult to admit that one is (perhaps) vain or greedy or lazy or worse. But it's even harder to honestly recognise the limits of one's virtues: am I kind, patient and generous (for example) as I would like to be? Or do I act kindly, patiently, generously only to those I love, only to those who please me, only when it suits me? That is not kindness or patience or generosity – it's just a form of self-interest! As C. S. Lewis has pointed out, real kindness, patience and generosity call on us to offer compassion to others in the light of *their* needs, whether we know them or not, whether we like them or not, whether it inconveniences us or not.[6] This is the compassion Jesus calls for when he says: "Love your enemies" (Luke 6:27). Real virtue is tougher than we like to think.

Who am I, Lord, that you love me? Often when we reflect on our character we find much that is good. No one is without any redeeming features, and many of us have a great deal to be honestly proud of! Nonetheless, there is generally room for improvement. And a surprising number of people find so very much fault in themselves that they feel unworthy of their own – let alone anyone else's – love or respect. Such low self-esteem is a miserable experience in its own right. Worse than this: it is a serious obstacle to spiritual development and the serenity that marks its fruition. For how can I feel comfortable, let alone happy, when I feel so disappointed in myself? And, convinced that I am flawed and weak, the challenge of growing into a strong spiritual identity can seem impossible, too difficult to even reach for.

Low self-esteem poses a real hurdle for development at any age, but perhaps especially as we retire, when all the usual props of our working lives fall away. Of course, in our hearts we know that our ultimate worth does not reflect what we have or have not achieved, nor even how good or bad a character we may have. Our ultimate worth is not reduced if we are no longer working or achieving, nor even if we have become weak and dependent on others or worse. Both the secular world and all the major religions proclaim that we are all, able or otherwise, good or bad, of equal and infinite value! Our worth is *unconditional,* and that is nothing less than our human birthright. As the prophet Isaiah put it, we are all *precious in God's eyes* (Isaiah 43:4). But it is not always easy to feel the peace and joy that ought to come from this news. The message that we are all of great worth *just as we are* is hard to take to heart when one is focused on one's failings. It's easy to feel that this message of joy applies to everyone else – but not to me…

Yet some people *can* acknowledge the weaknesses in their characters and simultaneously feel the joy, the high self-esteem that is our birthright. They can feel perfectly acceptable, just as they are, even though there may be a few warts to attend to. In fact, it's the peace and joy that come with this feeling of being perfectly acceptable that give them the space, the strength and desire to recognise and work to fix those warts. Their secret is simple: they judge themselves not as finished and unchangeable but as *works in progress*, travelling in the right direction and confident of reaching their destination, even though they have not reached it yet. These people have understood a wonderful truth: it is in our vulnerability, in our searching that we are most lovable, not in our perfection. *All heaven rejoices over a prodigal returned* (Luke 15:7).

The challenge of building a strong character rooted in the spiritual values of compassion and courage, justice and integrity begins with an honest appraisal of ourselves. And at the heart of this process is the challenge of self-esteem. Can we love ourselves *unconditionally?* Can we love ourselves, warts and all, as works in progress?

The invitation to grow

Who am I? In retirement, the labels we offer in answer to such questions are our names rather than our occupations. And whether we wish it or not, whoever we once were, character now matters more than activity or roles, titles or responsibilities in defining our identity. This more personal identity is both liberating and alarming! We are free to discover who we really are, now that the roles which have structured our lives have gone. But what if we don't like what we discover? Is it too late to answer the call to conversion, to meet the challenge of spiritual development?

Many people fear that at 50 or 60, 80 or 90 it is far too late to change in any fundamental way. Ancient lore has told us a thousand times that *leopards don't change their spots*, and we believe it. The popular press tells us that our basic characters are set by our genes, and what could possibly be done about that? But the fact is that psychologists are discovering that we are far more capable of change and development than we ever supposed, even in later life! Even in very old age.

What made you who you are? True, everything about us has a genetic basis, and many suppose that this fixes the basic shape of personality. But in reality genes have less control than the popular press might suggest. For example: most people believe that a baby with two X chromosomes will be a girl, a baby with an X and a Y chromosome will be a boy. Not necessarily so! It's actually the hormone testosterone that shapes a male body and brain – and the job of the Y chromosome is primarily to generate testosterone. High testosterone = male body; low testosterone = female body. But other things besides genes can disrupt the production or uptake of testosterone! Fluctuations in testosterone levels or sensitivity can mean that XX babies may be born as male bodies, or XY babies as female bodies. So even our gender is not wholly genetically determined! In fact, in every area of development, it is the *interaction* between our genes and experience which shapes us. And it's the opportunities which we explore, and the experiences we encounter, which go on shaping us throughout life. Our character is far from determined at birth, and is not set in stone, even in later life.

Our sense of self begins when we first see ourselves reflected in other people's eyes. A loving mother, for example, teaches her child that he or she is lovable, whereas a cold and unloving mother teaches the child that he or she is unlovable. A myriad of other relationships and interactions give us further information that shapes our understanding of who we are. We develop theories about ourselves – the theories that we call "personality" (for that is what personality is, an unconscious *theory*, albeit one that shapes our lives): *I am outgoing / shy; I embrace new experience / avoid it; I am conscientious / unreliable; I am lovable / unlovable; I am nervous / bold,* and so on. These theories shape how we react to experience and to others, and, in so doing, become self-fulfilling prophecies. For example, believing herself lovable and bold, Alice enters a new situation with confidence, expecting things to go well and to be liked. Her consequent open, agreeable behaviour elicits a positive response from others, confirming her beliefs about herself and reinforcing her confidence and charm. By contrast, believing herself unlovable and inept, Jane enters a new situation with tension and suspicion, expecting things to go badly and to be disliked. Her consequent dour, suspicious behaviour elicits a negative reaction from others, confirming her beliefs about herself and reinforcing her tension and suspicion. In sum, our own beliefs about ourselves create the consistency in our behaviour and experience!

If this is so, why does it seem so hard for people to change? In part, it's our belief that leopards can't change their spots, that we are genetically defined, which makes change seem impossible and not worth trying for. But the fact is that most of us don't really want to change. "Better the devil you know!" Better for things to stay just as they are, because in familiar patterns and situations we know what to expect and we know how to behave. This is why, for example, women who have been abused as children so often go on to marry abusive men, not just once, but over and over again: *better the devil you know.* And in our own, less dramatic way, each of us actively conspires to keep things – and ourselves – just the way they are, even if those things aren't satisfactory. We don't realise that we do it; but most of us, if we take the trouble to look, will find that we have made repeating patterns of choices that have kept us from changing much over the years.

And yet, real development and change are possible. It's hard to change while we are locked in familiar situations: there is too much strength of habit to overcome, and other people's expectations hold us where they are used to us being. But there is a very real possibility of change whenever we go through a major life transition: start school, for example, or begin a career, or marry – or retire. Such transitions shake us out of old patterns and bring new people with new expectations of us into our lives, freeing us to explore new ways of being. Often, of course, we spoil the chance of change by importing all our old habits and ways into the new situation, until others treat us exactly as everyone has in every situation before. But we could choose not to do that: we could choose to enter a new life stage, such as retirement, *deliberately open* to the possibility of growth and change, ready to try new ways of being, new ways of responding to others. We could make retirement a *turning point*, opening the door to real growth in character and spiritual strength, a shift from old habits to a new identity rooted in the eternal values.

A MEDITATION

Let us begin by centring ourselves: creating a space ready to reflect.

- Choose a time when you have at least a quarter of an hour to spare. Find a quiet place, as free from interruption and disruption as possible. Sit in a comfortable chair with your spine upright, your feet firmly on the floor, and your arms relaxed by your side. Close your eyes.

- Feel the tension in your feet and ankles, and let that tension go. Let your muscles relax, and feel the tension flow out from your feet and ankles to the earth. Now focus on your legs and do the same thing: feel the tension in your muscles and let it go. Now do the same thing with your hips, your spine, your chest, your arms and hands, your neck. Feel the tension around your jaw, your eyes; let it go and relax.

- Notice your breathing. Don't try to change it. Just listen to the rhythms of your body as you relax.

- Notice the sounds that come from outside and inside the room. And then go back to paying attention to your breathing.

- Sit quietly like this for a while. What is passing through your mind? Maybe there is nothing there except stillness. Or maybe you have some thought or image, or some emotion. Notice what it is and accept it; let it pass.

- How does it feel to let go of all the labels you have used to describe yourself in your working life, and stand "naked" in your character?

- How does it feel to explore what that character is?

- How would it feel to live in a character truly defined by the eternal values of compassion and courage, integrity and justice?

- Accept and acknowledge all your feelings and thoughts.

- Bring your attention back to your breathing and relax.

- And then gradually return to the world.

Retirement offers the opportunity and the invitation to embrace real spiritual development: the development of an identity rooted in values rather than work, in being rather than doing. The possibilities for growth, and for peace and joy through this growth are far greater than we suppose!

THE INVITATION OF CHRIST

Stay with us in meditative calm and listen to the word of God:

Retirement offers the opportunity and the invitation to embrace real spiritual development: to move beyond an identity defined by work to an identity rooted in spiritual values.

In a most comforting word God says to us, "even to your old age I am he, even when you turn grey I will carry you" (Isaiah 46:4).

God is doing for us in retirement what he did for us in our youth or in our years in the workplace – God is carrying us.

God who gave us life, throughout all our years, is giving us life right now and inviting us to become even more conscious that life is his gift. We may have asked many times, W*ho am I, Lord?* but we might have been too busy or too distracted to listen to the answer. In our time of retirement we have a new opportunity to hear the answer deep within our heart.

This is what God tells us about ourselves: we are made in the image and likeness of God (Genesis 1:26); we are fallen but redeemed (John 3:16); God says he made us "a little lower than God, and crowned... with glory and honour" (Psalm 8:5). Even when we sin God still assures us that we are precious in his sight (Isaiah 43:4). Jesus says we are "born of water and Spirit" (John 3:5). St Paul says, "your body is a temple of the Holy Spirit" (1 Corinthians 6:19). St Paul also says that we are God's work of art (Ephesians 2:10).

God's words to us about ourselves should fill us with amazement at our human dignity. *Who am I, Lord?* God says, you are my very image and likeness. *But who am I really, Lord?* God says, you are the temple of the Holy Spirit. You are an amazing mystery of God and God wants you to believe the truth about yourself, the truth that he reveals to you.

God pleads with us to accept our God-given dignity and worth. Indeed Pope John Paul II in his very first encyclical letter to all Christians said:

> In reality, the name for that deep amazement at human worth and dignity is the Gospel, that is to say: the Good News. It is also called Christianity. This amazement determines the Church's mission in the world and, perhaps even more so in the modern world.[7]

The truth of God's word to you about yourself doesn't depend on how you feel about yourself. God's word remains true even if you reject it and even if you feel that if God really knew you, as you think you know yourself, he wouldn't be saying these wonderful things about you.

Pope Benedict, in a very helpful word, says we must conform our minds to God's word.[8] We can, of course, conform – and maybe in the past we have conformed – our minds to somebody's negative word. We may have begun to see ourselves through the negativity of others rather than through the creativity of God. In retirement we have the opportunity to begin seeing ourselves as God does. We can, of course, continue to see ourselves in a negative way, refusing to believe in our hearts the word God speaks to us about ourselves. But we can also say: *From now on I am going to see myself as God sees me and I am going to accept myself as God accepts me.* It's our choice. But who sees us as we really are in God's sight? God or ourselves?

We can embark in retirement on a new path of self-acceptance; we can begin to cultivate good self-esteem; we can set out on an exciting new journey of spiritual development. Perhaps that is the reason why God has carried us to this stage of life. But negative thoughts about ourselves and our unworthiness can still stop us in our tracks. We may be feeling guilty about something in the past; we may even be condemning ourselves for some wrong turn we took in the past. God speaks to us directly, "Come now, let us argue it out, says the Lord: though your sins are like scarlet, they shall be like snow; though they are red like crimson, they shall become like wool" (Isaiah 1:18).

Let's take God at his word in our retirement and embark on a whole new spiritual development!

Notes

1   Personal communication to the authors.

2   Quoted in E. Katz, *Old Age Comes at a Bad Time* (London: Robson Books, 1997), 7.

3   B. Bettelheim, *The Informed Heart* (Harmondsworth: Penguin, 1991).

4   K. Monroe, *The Hand of Compassion: Portraits of Moral Choice During the Holocaust* (Princeton: Princeton University Press, 2006).

5   "Strangers to Ourselves", *The Psychologist*, 19 (2006), 600-603.

6   C.S. Lewis, *The Problem of Pain* (London: Zondervan, 2001).

7   John Paul II, *Redemptor Hominis*, 10.

8   Benedict XVI, *Jesus of Nazareth* (London: Bloomsbury, 2007).

4

Healing my life story

"... a good old age, full of days, riches..."
1 Chronicles 29:28

The early challenges of ageing are challenges of letting go: of facing
the necessary loss of youth and identity through our occupation, and
finding fulfilment in coming home to maturity in grateful acceptance.
We move on from the flower of youth to the fruits of maturity, fruits first
found in a strong personal identity, a moral character that transcends the
role we've played and the work we've done. But these challenges are
only the first of the spiritual tasks of ageing. They are the prelude to the
central task of maturity, when we look back on and make sense of our
life story as a whole.

The urge to make sense of our life story is strong as we move through
later life. Many people begin to reflect on their experiences, to
reminisce about times past, even to visit the places of childhood, youth
and adult life: the homes they once lived in, the schools they attended,
the places they worked, all places which have held important meaning.
This autobiographical journey seems to spring from an acceptance of
ageing, embracing the gifts of maturity. Certainly, it is enriched and
enlightened by the strength of character and the longer perspective that
maturity brings!

We can only make a coherent whole of our life stories from a mature
perspective. As we live through childhood, youth and busy adult life,
our understanding of that story is akin to that of someone reading a
detective novel: the clues and patterns are there as we go from chapter to
chapter, but we don't yet see them for what they are. It's only when we
begin to see how the story will end, that we recognise their significance
and start to make sense of them.

Reviewing our life story is a very useful exercise. In looking back we realise truths about ourselves which have eluded us until now. Sometimes they inspire us to engage with life with new joy, hope and energy! We see a life full of riches. But every human autobiography is a bitter-sweet affair; every human life has ups and downs. The spiritual challenge of maturity is coming to terms with *all* that we have experienced – or failed to experience.

The healing of grievances[1]

It's a rare human life that does not include some source of grief or grievance, some bitterness for things that have happened or been done to us. We can still suffer for the pain of a rejection in childhood or youth, for example, or burn with anger at the memory of an outrageous injustice ten years later. All of these painful memories come back as we review the story of our lives! How are we to deal with them?

The answer lies in healing memories through forgiveness. Every major religion in history has advocated forgiveness, not just as a spiritual grace but as a blessing for the forgiver as much as for the forgiven. Jesus calls his followers not just to forgive, but to become people whose lives are rooted in forgiveness, forgiving over and over again, "not seven times, but… seventy-seven times" (Matthew 18:22). And gradually, medicine and science are catching up with religion, and coming to see the healing power of forgiveness.

Why do we brood on grievances, hanging on to them for years, sometimes for ever? Usually, we are the only one hurt by it – the "villain" has long moved on and forgotten the event and is not affected by, or even aware of, our vengeful resentment. And yet we cling to our grievances, robbing ourselves of the peace and joy in our life story which are crucial to spiritual fulfilment and serenity. We believe that many people can't let go of grievances and embrace the healing power of forgiveness because they misunderstand the nature of forgiveness, and because they don't know how to go about the process of forgiving.

A man said recently to one of the authors: "I keep thinking that I have forgiven her... but then I remember it all again. I just can't forgive and forget." So many people are led astray by the adage "forgive and forget"! But forgiveness is *not* forgetting. There are things (the murder of a child, a husband's abandonment, the abuse of power by someone in authority, to name but a few) that we cannot, and should not, forget. Forgiveness is not about forgetting: quite the reverse. It's about coming to terms with reality. We don't pretend that nothing bad has happened when we forgive, nor do we let the offender off the hook. It is proper, even essential, to stand up for what is right and reject what is wrong. And it is right to expect those who have done harm to take responsibility for their actions and pay the penalty. It is the victim of harm, not the villain, who is set free by forgiveness: forgiveness is not letting go of the *offence*, but letting go of the *pain* which the offence has caused. Forgiveness brings emotional healing, stripping away the turmoil of outrage, the hurt and pain, and allowing us to feel at peace.

Many people would sympathise with the woman who said: "That's all very well. But I can't feel at peace if I have to ever again see the man who raped me, let alone live with him." She felt that she could never find peace in forgiveness because she could not bear reconciliation with her abusive father. But here is another misunderstanding. Forgiveness does not demand that we expose ourselves to further pain in any way. Forgiveness does not require reconciliation, or any further contact with those whom we have forgiven. This is acknowledged by every major religion in the world. Every religion urges us to forgive, not as a moral duty to others or even to God, but as a life-giving healing for ourselves!

But *how* do I go about forgiving and healing deep injuries from the past? Many people suppose that all we have to do is say, "I forgive", and the deed is done; but this is as absurd as imagining that one could become a skilled concert pianist simply by saying, "I will become a pianist"! Like mastering the piano, forgiveness is a process that needs effort. It's a process with many stages, which can sometimes occur in a flash, but which usually takes more time than we expect as we move slowly forward, or slip back to an earlier stage. It's a process which we generally don't understand, and so can't easily nurture. When we don't know where the process is going or why, it's easy to get stuck in one particular stage, perhaps for years; perhaps for ever.

Stage one – Denial

Forgiveness is seldom our first reaction to a grievance, though a few rare individuals seem to be stunned into it by the sheer immensity of their grief. More usually, our first reaction is denial: *this can't be happening!* It's as if the mind goes into shock, and defends itself by pretending that nothing bad has happened, or that what has happened doesn't matter. But this denial of reality cannot bring healing. In fact, it denies us all possibility of dealing with the hurt and anger.

Stage two – Self-blame

Strangely, the second stage in the process of forgiveness is *self-blame*. As we begin to accept the reality of our hurt, we accuse ourselves of having caused, or at the least having failed to prevent, the attack: *if only I had been a more lovable child / been a better wife / taken a different route home / made a different choice – this would not have happened to me!* Why do we blame ourselves, rather than others? This is another form of denial, another form of defence: if this is somehow *my* fault, then I could have kept safe by behaving differently. Believing this, however absurd that may be, means that we don't have to deal with the terrifying reality that our fate is not in our control. But this sense of safety is bought at the expense of adding the pain of self-punishment to the original injury.

Stage three – Victimhood

It's a step forward to move from self-blame to *victimhood*. Here is a healthy acknowledgement that this injury is not my fault, and not deserved! For the first time, the victim acknowledges that something very painful has happened, and that it was outside his or her control. The victim acknowledges a healthy vulnerability, and for the first time offers him or herself the compassion that every victim deserves. But it is easy to slip from here into an endless self-pity, a focus on the self which puts our problem wholly out of perspective. Wallowing in self-pity we forget that we are not unique in our suffering; that, in fact, suffering of equal or greater kind is a commonplace part of the human condition. Self-pity gives us an inward focus which directs us away from the real issues of acceptance and healing. It is a denial of our common humanity, a denial of our human capacity to transcend the rough and tumble of life. We have to let go of self-pity.

Stage four – Indignation

The fourth stage of forgiveness is *indignation.* How dare someone do this to me? Why should they get away with it? This anger is a healthy response, energising us to take action and interact afresh with the world where blank denial, self-blame and victimhood encourage passivity and withdrawal. At last, we are ready to stand up for ourselves and what is right! But this stage is problematic for many people who believe in forgiveness, since they often believe that we should achieve forgiveness without ever feeling anger. But in rejecting anger as intrinsically bad, these people cut themselves off from the further stages of forgiveness, and doom themselves to shuttle endlessly between self-pity, self-blame and denial. Anger is a natural, healthy reaction to outrage. Of course, anger that develops into hatred or vengeance is destructive – but there is no need for us to become locked in this negative cycle. Righteous indignation is the more balanced reaction, rejecting the offence and naming it as wrong, unfair and unjust. We need to acknowledge and honour this righteous anger so that we can deal with it on the journey to forgiveness.

Stage five – Surviving

Denial, self-blame, victimhood, indignation – these first four stages in the journey toward forgiveness are very natural reactions to assaults.

But none of them moves us on from the assault. Each, in its own way, locks us into the hurt, making it a central focus in our lives. It is only when we begin to let go of these feelings, and to re-engage with life in ways which are not defined by past injuries, that we begin to become true *survivors*, and to engage with the world with new purpose and hope. Psychologists expert in the process of forgiveness comment: "In the survivor stage you spend more and more time looking ahead toward health instead of back toward your pain."[2] We may have wished so many times that we could leave the hurts of the past behind! The survivor stage is when we begin to actually do that. This moving on is in many ways a healthy response, releasing us to live outside the shadow of our hurt again. Many people who reach this stage believe that they have reached full forgiveness and are healed! But this is not so. In the survivor stage we simply refuse to be dominated by past hurts, and put them aside to start life anew with a clean slate. But we are *not* starting with a fresh slate! All that has happened is still written on our hearts. Pushed aside, denied (however bravely), it lurks in the corners of memory, in subtle reminders that may suddenly catch us off guard and drag us back into indignation, self-pity, or self-blame. Thus this fifth stage in the journey to forgiveness is inherently unstable. And this is why so many of us believe that we can't achieve the healing of forgiveness! We mistake the survivor stage for full healing, when there is really far more, and far more important, work to do.

Stage six – Reintegration
To truly heal, to truly achieve the peace of forgiveness, we must let go of all forms of denial. We must accept and embrace all that has happened and understand how every little experience, good or bad, has contributed to who we are today. This sixth stage in the process of forgiveness, the stage of *reintegration*, challenges us to recognise, not only that we are the product of *all* our experiences – good or bad – but that good can come from bad – that, in fact, we grow more through suffering and setbacks than through sunshine and success.

Stage seven – Living in forgiveness

And if we can achieve this full integration of our story there is a peace, a spiritual fulfilment, a serenity that comes from accepting that our human journey is more complex and challenging than we would like it to be – and yet that there are riches which can *only* be found in that complexity and those challenges. And, in a profound way, to understand *me* at this level is also to understand *you*; and to understand is to forgive. This seventh stage of *being at peace with our whole life story* brings true healing and forgiveness. As we achieve insight into ourselves and others we find, often quite suddenly, that past grievances no longer have the power to distract or hurt us. We can contemplate them in serenity.

Achieving this seventh stage of forgiveness is possible, whatever age we are. This is the forgiveness advocated by all religions. It is the forgiveness which Jesus calls us to at every stage of life, deeply rooted in love: for ourselves and for others, even our enemies. To achieve it is a spiritual grace, whether we be young or old, believer or unbeliever. But healing our memories through forgiveness offers a special challenge and a special opportunity in later life, as we begin to look back over our whole story. As Gillian Rose wrote, reviewing her life as she came to terms with her imminent death from cancer: "To live, to love, is to be failed, to forgive, to have failed, to be forgiven, for ever and ever."[3]

As we review our life story we are likely to find many memories which need the healing of forgiveness. Forgiving is something we will be doing not once, but repeatedly. And in the process of integrating all the different hurts of life into our story, forgiving can become less a specific activity, more a way of being. This is the spiritual challenge of maturity: not merely to heal particular hurts, but to become *people who live in forgiveness*, people who bring the insightfulness of this highest stage of forgiveness not only to past memories, but to present situations as they happen too. Here is a wonderful foundation for spiritual fulfilment, and for serenity!

The healing of regrets

Perhaps even harder than healing the memories of all the bad things that have happened to us, is the challenge of healing the memories of all the things that we regret doing, and regret not having done. Such memories often begin to surface as we explore our characters, and make the transition from an identity based on our occupation, to something more personal.[4] Living with such regrets can be very painful. Self-criticism and disappointment can make us ill at ease with ourselves, and even lead us into self-loathing. Such spiritual malaise can cut us off, not only from comfort, but from all prospect of spiritual fulfilment.

Why is it so hard to forgive ourselves, or to feel the healing peace of being forgiven? Sometimes it's hard because those we have harmed are long gone from our lives. Or sometimes they are near but refuse to offer the forgiveness we long for. Sometimes we cannot feel forgiven, even when we are directly offered forgiveness: surely even God could not really forgive me for *that!* But in reality, it's only we who cannot forgive ourselves.

To live with the endless self-rejection that is at the heart of the inability to forgive ourselves is destructive. It does no good to anyone else, and it does us immense harm, robbing us of self-esteem and self-respect. It destroys our peace of mind and cuts us off from the confidence we need to reach spiritual fulfilment. We all need the healing of forgiveness.

Few of us have done anything truly terrible in our lives, even if there are things we bitterly regret. But even if we have done something really outrageous, we are not beyond forgiveness. Of course it is wrong simply to overlook misdeeds or wave them aside as if they do not matter. Forgiveness is not about letting anyone off the hook, not even ourselves. But our longing for forgiveness has nothing to do with being let off the hook, as if nothing bad had happened! In fact, it is our deep awareness of wrongdoing, our deep regret for it, which creates our yearning for forgiveness and our fear that we may be beyond it. And inherent in that regret is not only the wish that we had not done those things in the past, but the fervent desire never to do anything like that again. It is in this commitment to turning away from wrongdoing that we become worthy of forgiveness, even from ourselves. It is the courage to acknowledge our mistakes and to try to live a better life which makes us worthy of respect and love. As the psalmist expressed it, thousands of years ago:

> While I kept silence, my body wasted away
> through my groaning all day long…
> Then I acknowledged my sin to you,
> and I did not hide my iniquity;
> I said, "I will confess my
> transgressions to the Lord",
> and you forgave the guilt of my sin. (Psalm 32:3-5)

The gift of forgiveness is a vital blessing in every religion, bringing the gift of peace to our troubled consciences. Jesus says, to us all: "your sins are forgiven" (Matthew 9:2). Through Christ, we are promised forgiveness whether or not those we have offended forgive us. Through Christ, we are assured of God's forgiveness, whatever we may have done or failed to do, and however we struggle to live up to our intention of amendment: we will be forgiven not just *seventy times seven*, but *for ever and ever*. To accept this gift is to accept the gift of love. To love ourselves again is a spiritual grace in itself: for where is the virtue in loving our neighbours as ourselves if we can't even love ourselves? And to love myself sets me free to grow again, and to find the peace and joy of spiritual fulfilment.

But it's hard to feel forgiven, even with this glorious promise from God! We have known people who have found it so hard to believe that they can be forgiven that they have confessed the selfsame thing over and over, unable to accept the gift of absolution! Or people who believe somehow that the promise of God's forgiveness applies to everyone else, but not themselves. Here is, often, an extraordinary pride and vanity! (*I alone stand outside the ordinary constraints of human life, unforgivable where ordinary beings would be forgiven! I alone may condemn or redeem myself: not even God is an equal judge!*) Here is, often, a profound misunderstanding. Those who find it hard to feel forgiven expect forgiveness to come from *outside*, like a thunderbolt. Consumed by their own guilt, they wait for rescue. But to expect to be rescued from guilt while I myself bind it to me is as absurd as expecting someone else to take a ribbon from my hand when I have bound it inextricably to my fingers! To be free from guilt and shame we must be ready to let those things go. The truth is that, believer or unbeliever, we can only *feel* forgiven if we forgive ourselves! And forgiving ourselves means accepting ourselves just as we are, not yet ready for canonisation, but with a desire in our heart to do better. That desire is the gift of God and we should accept it as the surest sign of being forgiven. That desire to do better is a holy desire, and all holiness begins with a holy desire.

It is not just our misdeeds that we regret as we look back over a lifetime. Memory is also full of unfulfilled hopes. The words of a song by the Swedish group ABBA capture the sadness of letting go plans which can never now be fulfilled, and which tug our hearts:

> What happened to those wonderful adventures
> The places I had planned for us to go
> Well some of them we did but most we didn't
> And why I just don't know…
> Slipping through my fingers all the time.[5]

And then there is the regret that life has involved choices, the regret that we have taken some paths and not others. The poet T. S. Eliot expressed this regret for what might have been in the *Four Quartets*:

> Footfalls echo in the memory
> Down the passage which we did not take
> Towards the door we never opened
> Into the rose garden.[6]

Regrets of this kind do not call for forgiveness, for we have done nothing wrong. Rather, the problem is to come to terms with lost dreams, lost chances, lost possibilities – the things that we may feel we have missed out on. Who has not got a pocketful, if not a basket of such regrets, especially as we move into later life, when there seems to be so much more to regret?

For some, lost hopes and dreams fill their later years with an all-consuming sadness: they cannot see beyond the love they longed for and never had, or the adventure that never came their way, or the disappointment of some other hope. This malaise spoils the life they have! A core part of our search for spiritual maturity and serenity is to learn to cope with regrets and put them in perspective. But how?

The problem of regret is as old as time, and there is much popular wisdom on the subject – often from most unlikely sources! Many people have pointed out that we should *be careful what we wish for*, since it may not turn out the way we expect. What we have wished for and failed to find might not have brought us the happiness we hoped for, anyway! For example, in a competition to tell a story in six words, the writer Margaret Atwood captured the often misplaced hope that we place on relationships: "Longed for him. Got him. Shit"[7] – a sentiment that many a survivor of a failed marriage can share! Then there is the pragmatic advice to make the most of what we have, rather than demanding of life what it is not going to give – the Soviet leader Nikita Khrushchev offered the colourful advice that: "If one cannot catch the bird of paradise, better take a wet hen"![8]

This popular wisdom boils down to the suggestion that the only real way to deal with regrets is to accept life as it is. Hopes and dreams are just that: *hopes and dreams*, not reality. There could not possibly be time, in a single life, to fulfil all of the hopes and dreams that come to our hearts (we, who generally can't even finish all the urgent tasks on our daily to-do lists!). Many of us tend to focus on the dreams that got away rather than on the ones that came true, disposing ourselves toward sadness. Popular wisdom suggests the remedy: *count your blessings*.

Dealing with regret constructively is a key challenge for spiritual maturity. It demands real wisdom and courage to make sense of the way life has turned out: why we did not walk through certain doors, or how it happened that this or that hope was dashed, or fell by the wayside. In the words of the old prayer, we need "…serenity to accept the things I cannot change". Accepting our lives as they are is a major step on the journey to spiritual fulfilment.

Turning to joy

Letting go of grievances and regrets leaves us at peace with our life story. But peace alone is not enough to bring the serenity which is the mark of spiritual fulfilment: it needs the extra ingredient of joy.

How happy are you with the life you have led? Some people seem to live fairly privileged lives, while others seem to have a very great deal to put up with. But paradoxically, it isn't the people with the easiest lives who are the happiest! International comparisons have surprised researchers by revealing that we who live comfortable, safe lives in affluent Western societies are no happier – and indeed, often *less* happy – than people living in great poverty and insecurity in what we see as squalid slums, for all that our opportunities are so much greater, our health so much better, and that we and our children are so much more likely to live to old age!

Findings such as this are often used as evidence that material riches don't make us happy, and there is certainly truth in that: it is not the rich and famous who live the most fulfilled lives in our society, as newspaper stories constantly reveal. Money can't buy love or happiness, as every religion in the world has long taught. Indeed, the more we surround ourselves with material things, the emptier our lives may be.

But there is another reason why those who are less materially blessed may be happier with their lot. They may simply appreciate what they've got more! It's often when we are most aware of how precarious our lives really are that we appreciate them the most. For example, a brush with death on the roads can leave you shaken but feeling more gloriously alive than before; the threat of losing a job which has seemed mundane or stifling may make that job suddenly seem intensely desirable; a serious illness which threatens our life can make us appreciate just how happy we have been in a life that had seemed ordinary or even dull. As one woman, facing surgery for cancer, put it: "If I come through this, I shan't waste another moment sitting about feeling bored and lonely and fed up. Just give me my old life back and I shall savour every moment of it!"[9]

You can never tell, from the outside, what will make a human life feel rich and full and what will make it feel disappointingly empty. *Two men looking through prison bars. One sees mud, the other sees stars!* This old proverb captures a fundamental truth: it is not the life we have led which fills us with riches or leaves us empty – it's the approach we have taken to that life. One person may be filled with bitterness by an illness which leaves them only limping; another – such as Jane Campbell[10] – may say *life is sweet* though more or less wholly paralysed. In fact, it's striking just how many people whose lives appear to have been derailed by injury or illness or other misfortune say they would not undo those things if they could. Somehow they have found a greater richness in life since, and even *because of* it, than they ever had or expected before! Events which make us stop and reconsider what *really* matters often lead us to be thankful for the life we have, even if it may not look much to an outside view. Such events push us to develop a real spiritual strength rooted more truly in enduring values. And in living those values, we discover thankfulness.

We don't have to leave it until we are brought up short by some event to start considering what really matters and finding thankfulness in our lives. We can do this any time we choose. But reviewing our own story in later life is a clarion call to count our blessings and rejoice in the richness of our experience, whatever it has been! This is the positive route to take, from a purely psychological or medical point of view. Those who can accept life is as it is and find richness and joy in their life story are not only happier, but also often physically and emotionally healthier than those locked in disappointment, who can only see themselves struggling to make the most of a bad job (or worse). But more than this: thankfulness for the life we have been given opens a vital door to spiritual fulfilment and serenity.

Letting go of grievances and regrets leaves us at peace with our life story. But peace alone is not enough to bring the serenity which is the mark of spiritual fulfilment: that needs the extra ingredient of joy, as we noted at the start of this section. And we can find that joy only in thankfulness for our life. To truly feel such gratitude is immensely liberating: it suffuses us, not just with relief, but with ecstasy! We can *choose* to live in that thankfulness right now, whatever our circumstances may be, and there is no better way to start than with the prayer "I thank you for the wonder of myself."[11] The great Catholic mystic Meister Eckhart said: "if the only prayer you ever say in your whole life is 'thank you', that would be enough".[12]

A MEDITATION

Let us begin by centring ourselves: creating a space ready to reflect.

- Choose a time when you have at least a quarter of an hour to spare. Find a quiet place, as free from interruption and disruption as possible. Sit in a comfortable chair with your spine upright, your feet firmly on the floor, and your arms relaxed by your side. Close your eyes.

- Feel the tension in your feet and ankles, and let that tension go. Let your muscles relax, and feel the tension flow out from your feet and ankles to the earth. Now focus on your legs and do the same thing: feel the tension in your muscles and let it go. Now do the same thing with your hips, your spine, your chest, your arms and hands, your neck. Feel the tension around your jaw, your eyes; let it go and relax.

- Notice your breathing. Don't try to change it. Just listen to the rhythms of your body as you relax.

- Notice the sounds that come from outside and inside the room. And then go back to paying attention to your breathing.

- Sit quietly like this for a while. What is passing through your mind? Maybe there is nothing there except stillness. Or maybe you have some thought or image, or some emotion. Notice what it is and accept it; let it pass.

- What grievances are you harbouring? How would it feel to resolve those burdens and feel whole?

- How would it feel to let go of every regret and disappointment, and accept your life just as it is?

- How would waking to joyful thanksgiving for your life change your days?

- Accept and acknowledge all your feelings and thoughts.

- Bring your attention back to your breathing and relax.

- And then gradually return to the world.

The journey into age offers the possibility of looking back over the story of our lives, and finding patterns and themes which we may not have noticed before. Now is the time to heal old hurts, deal with regrets, wake up to how precious the life we have actually is! And in the process of doing this, we gain the healing peace of forgiveness, and the joy of thanksgiving: the peace and joy that are at the heart of spiritual fulfilment and serenity.

THE INVITATION OF CHRIST
Stay with us in meditative calm and listen to the word of God:

God invites us to the healing peace of forgiveness and the joy of thanksgiving for our life stories: the peace and joy that are at the heart of spiritual fulfilment and serenity.

Our life stories are whole and complete in God. Before even the world was made, God knew you. He didn't just begin to know you when you were conceived in your mother's womb or when you were born into this world. It was God who formed you in your mother's womb (Psalm 139:13) and as God said to Jeremiah: "Before I formed you in the womb I knew you, and before you were born I consecrated you" (Jeremiah 1:5). St Paul tells us that God: "chose us in Christ before the foundation of the world to be holy and blameless before him in love" (Ephesians 1:4).

We struggle with the notion of how God could know us before we were born. We often think that God only knows something about us as we live our daily lives – the things we do, our hopes and dreams, successes and failures. But (and this is the mystery) God knows everything about us, even before we were born. He knows not just our yesterdays and todays, but all our tomorrows. The psalmist also struggled and in the end said, "Such knowledge is too wonderful for me; it is so high that I cannot attain it" (Psalm 139:6).

Knowing everything about you, knowing everything that would happen in your life and how you would cope or fail to cope, God still lovingly created you. Long before you were a hope in your parents' heart, you were held in love in the heart of God. As the psalm says, "For it was you who formed my inward parts; you knit me together in my mother's womb. I praise you, for I am fearfully and wonderfully made. Wonderful are your works; that I know very well" (Psalm 139:13-14).

Gratitude to God for your creation, joy in being the person you are at this moment, are the necessary steps on the road to deeper faith and true serenity of heart. St Paul lists joy as the second fruit of the Holy Spirit: "the fruit of the Spirit is love, joy, peace, patience, kindness, generosity, faithfulness" (Galatians 5:22). Joy flowing from love is the characteristic mark of the Christian. Commenting on the words the angel spoke to Mary, "Greetings, favoured one! The Lord is with you" (Luke 1:28), Pope Benedict pointed out that "the first word of the New Testament is an invitation to joy".[13] Mary acted on that invitation. She told us in her magnificent song, "My soul magnifies the Lord, and my spirit rejoices in God my Saviour" (Luke 1:46-47).

The amazement at human dignity, at what God has done in us, fills the heart with joy, a joy that the troubles of this world cannot destroy. But the regrets and the sins, the hurts and the wounds of life can get in the way of fully opening our hearts in amazement and wonder at God's love for us. God reassures us: "I will sprinkle clean water upon you, and you shall be clean from all your uncleannesses, and from all your idols I will cleanse you" (Ezekiel 36:25).

God's gift of the "new heart" is the answer to all our troubles – the regrets or resentments about things in the past; the hurts others may have inflicted on us, or indeed that we may have inflicted on them; the loss of true perspective on the meaning and purpose of life. With the new heart from God we can heal our old hurts and forgive even our greatest enemies; with the new heart we can begin to live each day with enthusiasm and gratitude. We can confidently pray: "Create in me a clean heart, O God, and put a new and right spirit within me" (Psalm 51:10).

> The leitmotif of Christian spirituality is one of amazement at human dignity. This amazement fills us with joy in the realisation of being the beloved and redeemed sons and daughters of God. As Pope John Paul II said:
>
> We look back on the past with gratitude, we look forward to the future with confidence and live in the present with enthusiasm.[14]

Notes

1   This section and part of the next is based on J. McManus and S. Thornton, *Finding Forgiveness: Personal and Spiritual Perspectives* (Chawton: Redemptorist Publications, 2006).

2   Sidney and Suzanne Simon, *How to Make Peace With Your Past and Get on With Your Life* (New York: Warner Books, 1990).

3   G. Rose, *Love's Work* (London: Random Books, 1997).

4   See Chapter 3 above.

5   "Slipping Through my Fingers", 1981.

6   T.S. Eliot, *The Four Quartets* (Faber and Faber, 2001).

7   Quoted in L. Smith and R. Fershleiser (eds), *Not Quite What I Was Planning: Six-word Memoirs by Writers Famous and Obscure* (New York: Harper Perennial, 2008).

8   Quoted in *Time* magazine, 6 January 1958.

9   Personal communication to the authors.

10 See Chapter 2 above.

11 Our favourite morning prayer from Psalm 139.

12 Quoted in D. O'Neal (ed.), *Meister Eckhart, From Whom God Hid Nothing: Sermons, Writings and Sayings* (Boston: Shambhala Publications, 2005).

13 Benedict XVI, Homily at Mass for the Fourth Sunday of Advent, 18 December 2005.

14 John Paul II, *At the Beginning of the New Millennium*, 1.

5

Joy in the present moment

"Let everything that breathes praise the Lord!"
Psalm 150:6

The first two stages of development in later life – the stage of *letting go* of youth and of our occupations and embracing maturity and strength of character instead, and the *autobiographical* journey to healing and thankfulness – weave in and out, each contributing to the other as we draw nearer to old age. These are the processes which bring us wisdom and moral fortitude, the peace and joy which are the foundations of spiritual strength and serenity. But, even now, the journey to fulfilment is not complete: there's another step to take. The invitation to take that step is there, whatever stage of life we are at. But it is urgently signalled in three special challenges that we meet in the foothills of old age.

These three special challenges at the gates of old age seem, at first, very different. They are the challenge of coping with an ever-changing world; the challenge of coping with the loss of more and more of the people we've loved; and the challenge of coping as time starts running out. But the developmental invitation is the same for all three: it is the challenge to live joyfully in the present moment. And this is not simply a practical solution, as we shall see in this chapter, it is also a powerful spiritual grace – the step which brings serenity to full fruition.

A changing world
We may achieve inner stillness through the first two stages of development in later life, but the busy world keeps changing around us all the time – and somehow we have to live with that! Everything keeps changing, from political issues to fashions, from views on what is or isn't socially acceptable to basic manners, and then there are

astonishing technological advances which seem to continually change how we watch television, use phones or find information...

In youth and through our working days we keep more or less abreast of all this change, seeing it as a natural and even desirable progress. The children we live with, the people we work with, even the demands of the work we do, combine to keep us up to date. But as we move through retirement we begin to lose touch with that busy world. More and more we find ourselves surrounded by new-fangled and sometimes baffling gadgets and gizmos, new and perhaps worrying manners and lifestyles. We can easily find ourselves drifting further and further out of step with the world around us, wrapped in disapproval. A well-known fridge magnet asserts that, "middle age is when a broad mind and a narrow waist swap places" – and all too often that's the truth! All of this presents us with a challenge that is both material and spiritual.

The material challenge is to *manage* in this brave new world: to find a way through the complexities of an ever-changing life and to stay connected with the world around us. This makes sense from a purely practical point of view. It's hard to function if we're out of step with the world. It's far easier to at least try to master the new technology, the new ways of living, than to swim against the tide. Psychologists find, too, that people who stay more closely connected to modern life are likely to be physically and emotionally healthier than those who are alienated. Alienation is an inherently negative state, associated with depression and isolation. It's the very opposite of the love of life that the French call *joie de vivre*.

Of course it would not be healthy to go along with *every* changing aspect of life! Some things that shape the modern world are simply irrelevant to us in later life (for example, the fashions of youth culture). And some aspects of the modern world reflect a spiritual emptiness, even a moral bankruptcy which it is absolutely right to reject (the binge-drinking that is fashionable with the young, for example, or the television programmes that humiliate people for amusement). The spiritual challenge is to stay focused in our values: to reject things from positive strength of character because they are inappropriate for us or morally wrong, rather than simply rejecting things in disgruntled negativity simply because they are new.

The material and spiritual challenges of a changing world combine in calling us to *stay engaged* as we age: to stay joyfully connected to the world as it is, rather than losing ourselves in nostalgic regret for the way things used to be – a regret that is anyway more often founded in imagination than reality (as the writer Margaret Atwood put it: "I've never understood why people consider youth a time of freedom and joy. It's probably because they have forgotten their own"). And inherent in this challenge is the key idea of living in the present: to become people who engage life as it is, rather than life as it once may have been.

Changing relationships

Changing practicalities, social manners and technology can challenge a serene old age, but that is as nothing to the challenge posed by changes in our personal lives. Children grow up and leave home to live their own adult lives, becoming visitors to ours. Marriages and friendships may dissolve in misunderstanding or recrimination, broken by the strains of human interaction, or simply fade into silence. Colleagues we once saw every day slip out of our lives as we retire. Friends and neighbours move away – or we move away from them – and daily contact is reduced to occasional visits, phone calls, and cards at Christmas. Our parents, aunts and uncles die, and we are orphaned, no matter how old we may be. And then brothers, sisters, beloved husbands or wives – friends we have shared a lifetime with – begin to die. And this is a serious challenge at many levels.

The longer we live, the more likely it is that we will be the last survivor of a group of friends or relatives, which can be a very lonely thing. As one old lady in a nursing home said: "There's no one left, now, who calls me Nellie as everyone did when I was a girl. Now it's Mrs Wilson. Or if I'm lucky, Elizabeth." No one can replace the people we've shared our youth with, or who have been part of the warp and woof of our days as we grew through adult life and into retirement. It's not just that it takes years for a friend to become an utterly trusted confidant, though that's often the case. It's also that there is something very special about the relationships we form in youth and adult life. As we lose those people, there is no one left to laugh over old stories or share the memory of some old triumph or disaster.

It's easy, as we grow older and lose more and more of the people we have loved, to become isolated and feel lonely and abandoned. Focusing on lost relationships it is easy to become depressed and withdrawn. The poet Henry Vaughan expressed the sadness of this:

> They are all gone
> into the world of light,
> and I alone sit
> lingering here.[1]

But, of course, we are not really alone. Unless we choose to live in seclusion (and even then, in these days of instant communication) we are surrounded by people, even if they might not be the people we'd wish to have around us. The challenge of later life is to make connections with new people – and again, it is both a material and a spiritual challenge.

We are a sociable species. Isolated, some of us unravel – and even the best of us tend to go a little strange! We need human company and, more than that, we need love if we are to thrive. One of the best predictors of a long and healthy life is the quality of our relationships. So from a purely practical point of view, the healthy response as old relationships end is to reach out to make new connections with new people. It's in our own best self-interest! But the spiritual challenge is to do far more than merely reach out for help and support. It is to offer our own gift of self – in other words, our own gift of love to others, too. This gift of self, that reaches out in solidarity rather than self-centredness, is a powerful spiritual grace.

The song says: "if you can't be with the one you love, love the one you're with".[2] The cure for loneliness and isolation is not waiting to be loved, it is offering love to others. As those we've loved slip out of our lives, the material and the spiritual challenge is to continue to reach out to connect in love with others all our days, rather than letting our capacity to love slip away. Again, the challenge is to live in the present moment, rather than the past: to become people joyfully engaging with others in present love, rather than rooted in past loves.

It would be hard to overstate the spiritual importance of this reaching out to others in love. None of us will flourish without it! As Pope John Paul II said:

> Men and women cannot live without love. They remain beings that are incomprehensible for themselves, their lives are senseless, if love is not revealed to them, if they do not encounter love, if they do not experience it and make it their own, if they do not participate intimately in it.[3]

Indeed the Church teaches that it is only in making the sincere gift of self in love that we can find our true selves.[4] Each person has that capacity to make the sincere gift of self in love to the other. Pope John Paul defined this capacity in this way:

> the power to express love: precisely that love in which the human person becomes a gift – and through this gift – fulfils the very meaning of his or her being and existence.[5]

The person who is reaching out in love, making a sincere gift of self to the other, is fulfilling his or her existence, no matter what else may be happening in his or her life.

Shrinking time

As if it weren't enough that the world and the people we connect with change around us as we age, even time starts to change...

Everybody's grandmother has probably warned that time goes faster and faster as we get older – and so it does. Where Sunday afternoon stretched out like eternity in childhood, whole years seem to flash by in the blink of an eye as we age! And time doesn't just go faster: it starts running out. Bill Clinton commented at the end of his term as US President, "Suddenly there are more yesterdays than tomorrows."[6] And most of us can agree with the anonymous contributor to the competition to tell a life story in six words, who wrote: "I thought there'd be more time."[7]

Why does time seem to speed up and run out in this extraordinary way as we get older? There are many psychological theories, which explore the way that busyness or idleness affects our experience of time passing – or the way a deadline seems to make time pass more quickly. These theories point to the fact that how we experience time depends on how we use it.

The truth, of course, is that time doesn't change as we age: a moment is a moment, whether we are eight or 80. What changes is our relationship with time. Young children live intensely in each moment, forgetting the past and unconcerned with the future. They live with the feeling of having all the time in the world! We in later life normally live anywhere but in the present moment: we live in memories of times past, in hopes or fears for the future. We scarcely even notice the moment we're in, let alone inhabit it intensely! Small wonder that we lose our sense of the gift of time. Small wonder that we wake up to notice that whole days seem to have shot by in a second, while our minds were wandering in memories, or fretting about the future. Small wonder that we feel the future is shrinking as we focus on our great age rather than on the moment!

The sensation of time slipping away is painful, even frightening to many people. Life itself seems to be slipping away! And here again is both a practical and a spiritual challenge. The invitation is to use time differently. From a practical point of view, the way to experience time as we did in childhood is to live in it as we did in childhood: in other words, to live intensely in each moment, unconcerned with the past or the future. Now, we can directly experience the fullness of each moment so that time is on our side again: only this precious moment matters.

But living intensely in the present moment in this way is far more than a practical solution to our changing perception of time! In fact, it is a powerful spiritual grace. So much of our lives is spent living in the mists of memory or the mysteries of the uncertain future! We are like people beside a beautiful waterfall, standing with our eyes firmly fixed on our notes and guidebooks, rather than looking at the waterfall we have come to see! A flower remembered, a flower imagined, never has the richness of a flower directly experienced. Only what is here in the present moment is real. Only by being fully aware in this present moment can we *be truly alive, or begin to have life, and life more abundantly* (John 10:10).

Serenity in the present moment

The three special challenges at the gates to old age combine to invite us to engage the present world rather than wandering in past ways, to love those near us in the moment rather than living in mourning for lost loves, and to live intensely in the present moment rather than in memory or an imagined future. There is obvious spiritual wisdom in this – but what has it to do with serenity? What has it to do with the journey of development into old age, which we explored in the previous chapters?

In his immensely popular book *The Power of Now*,[8] Eckhart Tolle argues that serenity will spring from living in the present moment. To live fully in the present moment is to live without regret for the past, without fear for the future: free to live this moment in the tranquil joyfulness that is the peace that passes all understanding (Philippians 4:7) – the peace of God. Some people can simply step into the present moment and live there in serenity forever, catapulted into it by some crucial experience. Eckhart Tolle himself seems to have found serenity in just this way – suddenly, overnight, transformed from a man in crisis and despair to an extraordinary serenity and presence which has never left him. But few people find serenity in this way, and, even if we do, it is often a fragile serenity that may be ambushed by regret or hope at any moment, as this letter shows:

> I'd been in a dreadful state, heart-broken and confused, my life in ruins. I was too anxious and distressed to manage even everyday things like booking a train ticket. Then one day while I was staying with a friend, I was unexpectedly overcome by the strong sensation that everything was going to be fine. It wasn't that I expected all my problems to be solved: it was that all the fear and anxiety for the future, the regret and anguish over the past suddenly went away. I was filled with an astonishing, joyful peace! I felt the presence of God. I slept for hours, most of the next day. And when I woke, that marvellous peace, that powerful sense of God's presence was with me. And it stayed with me for nearly a year. But gradually, as everyday problems mounted up, I fell back into worrying about the future, ruminating on the past. And one day, that wonderful serenity had gone. And I had no idea what to do to get it back.[9]

Very few people ever have the experience of a sudden serenity as this woman did. Most people have to work for it. And most don't know how to do that work. Can one simply decide to live in the present moment, and expect to find serenity there? Simply being vividly focused in *this* present moment, with no thought for the past or plan for the future, is not necessarily enough to fill us with serenity – as any sailor battling around rocks in a storm can tell you! Sometimes we are vividly present in a moment that is anything but peaceful or joyful.

Finding serenity in the present moment requires more than simply forgetting the past and the future: it means healing and coming to terms with the past and coming to a complete acceptance of ourselves just as we are, warts and all – not a write-off, but a work in joyful progress. It's possible to do that at any age. But the spiritual challenges of later life which we have explored in this book point very directly to the path through which each and every one of us can work our way towards serenity.

As we work to come home to our human bodies – to develop and embrace our true identity, heal the grievances and regrets of our life stories, and come to joyful thankfulness for the lives we have lived – we actively come to terms with ourselves and our life stories. We lay firm foundations for the peace and joy which are essential for serenity: strong foundations rooted in awareness rather than forgetting; able to transcend the regrets of the past. And as we accept the challenge of living in the present moment, we bring the peace and joy of this serenity into our lived experience: *now* we are *living* in serenity, not just laying its foundations! And in this lived experience there is new treasure: we come to peace not only with the past and the present, but also with the future.

Finding transcendent serenity

As we have seen through the course of this book, the journey to serenity is a journey to spiritual strength, built on fundamental values. As we begin to live in serenity in the present moment, we begin to live those values from moment to moment in a spirituality that is wholly integrated into every part of life. Spirituality becomes a matter of *being*, not something we *do* now and then. It permeates our every thought, experience, action. This is true spiritual fulfilment.

Psychologists tell us that the ability to truly live in the peace and joy of serenity in the present moment is a major component of good mental health. Every religion urges us to live in serenity in the present moment:

in other words, to live *always* in serenity, all of the time. For every major world religion and for many ancient and modern philosophies, a life lived in serene presence in the moment is spiritual grace in and of itself, the achievement of life's purpose. This is what saints and mystics aspire to. This is the presence which so impresses us in those we recognise as spiritually fulfilled. This is the spiritual fulfilment that every one of us can reach.

And everything changes when we truly live in serenity in each moment. This is not *mindless* peace but an intensely *mindful* presence! This is not a fatalistic acceptance of life, but a joyous consent to be exactly where we are, exactly who we are – come what may.

When we truly live in serene presence in each moment, we bring all the resources of our spiritual *being* to bear in each and every moment. The path which has led us here is the path of awareness and honesty, courage and integrity, compassion and justice. We bring all of those strengths and virtues to bear in experiencing and making sense of each moment, fully mindful and fully present. We are fully centred, aware and at peace wherever we may be, because we are fully focused on eternal spiritual values and not on the ephemera of the material world.

> All shall be well, and all shall be well,
> And all manner of things shall be well.[10]

Julian of Norwich's ecstatic song of serenity expresses the powerful and positive acceptance of life which comes with living in mindful spiritual presence in the moment. Those who have experienced this feeling will know that it reflects anything but a childish expectation that the problems of the world will be magically fixed, or that we will be spared suffering or pain. And they will know that this feeling is anything but a passive resignation to fate, whatever that may be. But these things are a mystery to those who have not yet experienced this blessing.

The Christian prayer of serenity is:

> God, grant me the serenity to accept the things I cannot change; courage to change the things I can; and wisdom to know the difference.[11]

It is in living this prayer moment by moment that we live our spiritual strength. We don't abandon our responsibilities for the world or others, or for our own actions and welfare: we will do our best. But if we really cannot change things, then we will accept that reality: we will consent to be here, even if "here" is very far from what we would have chosen. Not to consent is pointless. What do we gain by raging against the inevitable, apart from stress? Nothing, as many a person has discovered to their cost. Those who truly live in serenity in the moment stand by the spiritual values that are the foundations of serenity, even when facing disaster. We don't pretend that the situation is good, and we don't give up on life in such circumstances: rather, we embrace the gifts of life, the spiritual gifts of serenity which are still there for us no matter what may be happening. It is in this way that we feel that *all shall be well, and all shall be well, and all manner of things shall be well.* It is not the situation but *I*, my spiritual *being,* which shall be well. And here we build the final foundation for a truly transcendent serenity: for here we come to peace, not only with the past and the present, but also with the future, *come what may.*

For the Christian, this true transcendental serenity has a special dimension: we consent to whatever may come, not merely confident in the strength of our own being, but placing ourselves in the hands of God. As Jean-Pierre de Caussade put it, we abandon ourselves joyfully to divine providence: *Your will be done, O Lord; not mine.*[12] In such prayers we submit our individual will to the will of God in absolute trust: *into your hands, Lord, I commend my spirit.* What is it that we trust in? Not some sort of material rescue! Christ was not rescued from his cross, and we don't expect to be rescued from ours. Rather, we place ourselves in God's care, confident in Jesus' promise: "I am with you always, to the end of the age" (Matthew 28:20). We trust that wherever we are, we are not beyond the love of God, and not beyond sacred meaning and purpose. We are part of life, and precious in the essence of life that we call God. We place our lives in God's care trusting that we matter, and are utterly safe in that mattering. Our prayer of trust is as small, as immense as: *Lord, never let me go.*

The sacred moment

To the Christian, the present moment is sacred. This is an idea that is familiar to other religious traditions, such as Judaism and Islam. God lives in the present moment. And even for those who don't believe in our God, there is something sacred and numinous about the experience of being serene and present in the moment, something that connects us to a reality far beyond our limited individual horizon.

Why should God inhabit the present moment? But where else could the essence, the life-force of our universe be? Not in the confabulations of our human memories, nor in the fantasies of our imagined futures! God can *only* be found in the reality of the present moment. And yet, how could a creator God be limited by time?

The time we understand is *chronos*: the time of chronologies, of chronographs – *clock time.* (But in fact we don't even really understand that, as Einstein pointed out: chronological time is apparently not a fixed constant as we suppose. Fly to the stars, fly even from Europe to America, and chronological time passes differently for the flier and the earthbound. It's an idea well explored in science fiction, where those brave enough to commit two years of lived time to a flight at unimaginable speed to another planet return to find that a hundred years have passed on earth.) We live in clock time as we understand it, a whirling world of plans, diaries and appointments, of deadlines passed, deadlines to come; a world that is far less stable, measurable, quantifiable or predictable than we suppose.

Even we, who know so little of the true nature of God, know enough to understand that God cannot live in *chronos*! Not in our chronically disorganised, chronically stressed, chronically limited conception of time. The ancients knew that there is another dimension to time: *kairos*. Here time is not parcelled out in finite units. Here, each moment stretches for infinity. Here, every infinite moment is filled with the presence of God. When we live a full spirituality in the present moment, we enter *kairos*: God's time. And here is a time when peace and joy are magnified beyond all expectation!

When we live in *kairos*, we live in the presence of God. Here is a blessing which magnifies all the fruits of our labours to live in serenity! Here, finally, is the peace that passes all understanding: the peace of God. It's there for all of us, whatever we may or may not believe (we do not create God by our beliefs, nor un-create God by disbelief – what a vanity!). No theology, no credo can guarantee awareness of the presence of God. But if you live in the moment in a powerful, transcendental serenity; if your experience is then suffused with glory, with overpowering peace and joy, with overflowing love; *now* you are living in the presence of God!

A MEDITATION

Let us begin by centring ourselves: creating a space ready to reflect.

- Choose a time when you have at least a quarter of an hour to spare. Find a quiet place, as free from interruption and disruption as possible. Sit in a comfortable chair with your spine upright, your feet firmly on the floor, and your arms relaxed by your side. Close your eyes.

- Feel the tension in your feet and ankles, and let that tension go. Let your muscles relax, and feel the tension flow out from your feet and ankles to the earth. Now focus on your legs and do the same thing: feel the tension in your muscles and let it go. Now do the same thing with your hips, your spine, your chest, your arms and hands, your neck. Feel the tension around your jaw, your eyes; let it go and relax.

- Notice your breathing. Don't try to change it. Just listen to the rhythms of your body as you relax.

- Notice the sounds that come from outside and inside the room. And then go back to paying attention to your breathing.

- Sit quietly like this for a while. What is passing through your mind? Maybe there is nothing there except stillness. Or maybe you have some thought or image, or some emotion. Notice what it is and accept it; let it pass.

- Do you consent, without reservation, to be exactly who you are, where you are, whatever may be happening in life?

- What does it feel like to be fully present in, fully accepting of this moment?

- Gather up the peace and joy of the moment; feel it through your body, your mind, your soul. Feel the union with the pervading power of the universe that we call God!

- Accept and acknowledge all your feelings and thoughts.

- Bring your attention back to your breathing and relax.

- And then gradually return to the world.

The final stage of development in later life is the stage of spiritual fulfilment: where we at last begin to live in transcendent serenity moment by moment, and always. Finally we consent utterly to live our lives fully, in peace and joy, in the peace of God that passes all understanding. Finally we can *be still and know God* (Psalm 46:10).

THE INVITATION OF CHRIST

Stay with us in meditative calm and listen to the word of God:

This is the moment the Lord gives us: the gift of *kairos*, in which moment we find God.

Jesus begins his preaching with the words, "The time is fulfilled, and the kingdom of God has come near; repent, and believe in the good news" (Mark 1:15). We can only respond to Christ in the present moment. We can't repent and believe yesterday, nor tomorrow. The invitation is given to us today and we can only accept it in the now, in the present moment, in the *kairos* moment. Scripture is very insistent on this: "O that today you would listen to his voice! Do not harden your hearts" (Psalm 95:7-8). God's moment, God's hour of salvation has come and we are invited to live in this hour.

The mystics taught that God is closer to us than we are to ourselves. St Paul said that it is in God that we "live and move and have our being" (Acts 17:28). God's kingdom is here and now, – even though we can't see it with our physical eyes, we see it with the eye of faith, the eye of the heart. Jesus says, "the kingdom of God is among you" (Luke 17:21).

How do we respond to this glorious truth? First, in awareness that we can never be completely alone. As Jesus said, "I am with you always" (Matthew 28:20). His presence deepens the secure stillness, the peace and joy of our serenity. And our response to this is gratitude and praise!

Even the wonders of the natural world excite our praise. One evening one of the authors, Jim, was sitting with hundreds of people at the Grand Canyon, waiting for the sun to go down. Jim recalls that the whole crowd was reduced to silence as the light began to change and the great cavity of the canyon filled up with an amazing kaleidoscope of brilliant hues. From that vast crowd there came forth just one word, *Wow*. That was praise, amazement at the pure beauty unfolding before the crowd! How much more does our amazement at the presence of God move us to praise?

St Augustine expressed it this way: "You arouse us to take joy in praising you, for you have made us for yourself, O Lord, and our heart is restless until it rests in you."[13] In this present moment our heart can find rest in God! Our praise is God's gift to us, not ours to him. As we say in one of the Prefaces at Mass: "You have no need of our praise, yet our desire to thank you is itself your gift." It is through our heartfelt thanksgiving and praise that we find rest in God. And it is our whole being that responds in praise to God! As the psalmist prayed, "Bless the Lord, O my soul, and all that is within me, bless his holy name" (Psalm 103:1).

At any moment of any day we can enter into our own hearts and become aware of the deep mystery of God's presence within us and speak our words of praise. And so we can live joyfully in the kingdom of God as we age, and find a rich fulfilment for our whole life.

The great mystic Meister Eckhart said if the only prayer you said in your whole life was "thank you", you would have prayed very well. So now, at this moment, you can pray very well! All you have to do is to recall that God is with you, within you and indeed all around you, and say *thank you*.

Notes

1   Quoted in E. Katz, *Old Age Comes at a Bad Time* (London: Robson Books, 1997), 45.

2   Stephen Stills: "Love The One You're With".

3   John Paul II; *Redemptor Hominis* (London: CTS, 1979), 10.

4   Second Vatican Council, *Gaudium et Spes*, 24.

5   John Paul II, *Man and Woman He Created Them: A Theology of the Body*, trans. Michael Waldstein (Boston: Pauline Books & Media, 2006), 15.1.

6   Quoted in E. Katz, *Old Age Comes at a Bad Time* (London: Robson Books, 1997), 63.

7   Quoted in L. Smith and R. Fershleiser (eds), *Not Quite What I was Planning: Six-word Memoirs by Writers Famous and Obscure* (New York: Harper Perennial, 2008).

8   E. Tolle, *The Power of Now: A Guide to Spiritual Enlightenment* (London: Hodder & Stoughton, 1999).

9   Personal communication to the authors.

10 Julian of Norwich, *Revelations of Divine Love*.

11 Attributed to the American theologian Reinhold Niebuhr.

12 J. P. de Caussade, *The Sacrament of the Present Moment* (London: HarperCollins, 1989).

13 *The Confessions of St Augustine* (New York: Doubleday, 1960), book 1, chapter 1.

6

Last things

"Even though I walk through the darkest valley, I fear no evil."
Psalm 23:4

Our society isn't good at handling the final challenges of life. We live in fear of physical illness, investing huge effort in staying well or, if that fails, searching for cures for our ills. We live in terror of dementia, the seeping away of memory and intelligence, and eventually even the basic skills of independent life. We dread death, fighting it as the ultimate enemy. Not for nothing is Dylan Thomas' cry of protest one of the most quoted of all passages of poetry:

> Do not go gentle into that good night,
> Old age should burn and rave at close of day;
> Rage, rage against the dying of the light.[1]

And we tend to share the comedian Woody Allen's sentiment: "I don't want to achieve immortality through my work. I want to achieve immortality by not dying."[2] There are some among the super-rich who spend millions searching for personal immortality, even having their bodies frozen to await the dawn of some future science which might one day bring them back to life.

The fact is that death and the various illnesses which often precede it are a natural part of the human condition. Some may escape the trials that these things can impose by dying suddenly and unexpectedly, perhaps in their sleep or from an illness that has lurked secretly, with no symptoms to give it away, in the darkness of the body. It's tempting to wish for such an easy end! But such "easy" death is not without price: by its very nature, sudden and unexpected death very often comes before we have had time to complete our human responsibilities, let alone develop our full spiritual potential. It allows no time to prepare ourselves or anyone else. Perhaps facing the trials of a final illness, as most of us do, has some blessings.

What consolation can spirituality offer us in the last days of life? For the Christian, death offers the ultimate consolation of Christ's promise that there is a life beyond this earthly life, in which we shall be reunited with all those we have loved and, above all, with God. But even among the faithful, this promise of resurrection doesn't fill all our needs. Believer or unbeliever, we will all have to face the challenge of the last days of our life in this world. We need spiritual consolation here, now, to help us find a way through.

What consolation can we find in a life lived in transcendent serenity in the present moment, in spiritual being, as we face the challenge of last things? Serenity seems to meet its hardest test as we come to the end of our lives. But extraordinarily, wonderfully, some people only find this transcendent peace as they meet this last test.

Consolation for a fading mind

A sticker on a pot on Stephanie's desk reads: "Of all the things I've lost, I miss my mind the most" – over the years it has become less amusing! As we grow older we begin to watch ourselves anxiously for signs of a fading mind. Each time we walk upstairs to fetch... whatever it was... and come down empty-handed, each time we lose our glasses and find them on top of our head after turning half the house upside down, or forget the name of a familiar face, or add two and two and make six, or fumble some familiar skill, we worry. Of course, we've actually been making mistakes like these all our lives! It's only now that we start to read something sinister into it. Memory is far less reliable than we suppose, even in our adult prime, as the song reminds us:

> We met at nine (we met at eight)
> I was on time (no, you were late)
> Ah yes! I remember it well!

We dined with friends (no, we were alone)
A tenor sang (a baritone)
Ah yes! I remember it well! ("I Remember It Well", from *Gigi* [3])

The memory loss of dementia is gradual. It takes a long time, perhaps years, for memory to become seriously disrupted, seriously different from the normal. Such problems are on the rise. This is the price we pay for our longer lives: 50 years ago few people lived into their 80s, and so dementia was rare. Today so many live way past 80 that even village shops carry several different designs of hundredth-birthday card! Perhaps there is nothing in old age that we fear so much as the possibility of losing our minds to this terrible family of diseases. Many of us won't: even at 100, many minds are still sharp and bright. But some of us will face the loss of our memories and intelligence, the things which seem to carry our personality.

The author Terry Pratchett was diagnosed with Alzheimer's disease at the unusually early age of 59. With enormous courage he allowed film-makers to make a documentary of his search, first for a cure, and then for ways to live as he would become less and less able to manage for himself. It was heartbreaking to see a man of such extraordinary wit and intelligence becoming helplessly unable to tie his own tie, type his own work, or read aloud from his own novel. But it was uplifting to watch, too. In his conversations with other sufferers in the early stages of disease, in his visits to nursing homes for those whose minds had faded much further, in his identification with all these people, he managed to remind us that, for all their memory problems and disabilities, these people are as alive, as significant, as precious as any of the rest of us. And that's a message that those facing dementia very much need to hear.[4]

We fear many things about dementia. Perhaps, for many of us, the greatest fear is that as our memories become vague and our competence declines we shall somehow lose our humanity. But this fear is groundless. Our humanity, and our value and worth have nothing to do with our intelligence, competence or independence. The brightest and best of minds may achieve more than others and be more useful than others (though history suggests that there is no guarantee of this!), but their intrinsic human worth is no greater. The least bright, the most intellectually disabled child is as precious, as valued, as fully human as any other, both in the eyes of God and in the eyes of society. Indeed, the measure by which we judge the spiritual health of a society is how it reacts to the least gifted and most vulnerable of its members: with love and care, or disregard and abandonment? We are a people committed to compassion and respect for *all*, from the strongest to the frailest, from the brightest to the least bright. We cannot lose one jot of our humanity, no matter how frail our brains may be or become. The art is truly believing that this applies, not just to others, but even to *me*.

The consolation that spiritual strength in serenity offers, in the face of a fading mind, is captured in the serenity prayer which applies to every aspect of life:

> God, grant me the serenity to accept the things I cannot change; courage to change the things I can; and wisdom to know the difference.[5]

Faced with a diagnosis of some sort of dementia, we need courage. It is right to do all that we can to nurture our minds, whether they be strong or frail. And there is much that we can do. Medicine is making new discoveries every day. There are already drugs which can slow the progress of memory loss and boost general intelligence. Some experts believe that within five or ten years we may have drugs which can halt or even reverse the effects of cognitive decline, perhaps cure diseases like Alzheimer's. Furthermore, recent discoveries in science hold out the hope that we may sometimes be able to slow the progress of memory loss through the way we use our brains. Studies of recovering alcoholics, who very often have marked damage to the memory and ability to think and plan, suggest that good nutrition, stimulating the mind and exercise (which floods the brain with oxygen) help in the recovery of memory and reasoning. Brain cells destroyed by alcohol are gradually replaced. Where once we believed that we are born with every brain cell we shall ever have, so that every loss is irreplaceable, we now know that new brain cells continue to form right through our lives: the more so the more we nurture and use our brains! And even if we cannot stem the tide of memory loss, there are many things that we can do to cope – from pinning up reminders, to recruiting companions to help with those things we can no longer do alone.

Viewed from outside, the darkness of severe memory loss can seem unfathomably deep. But scientists are discovering that, viewed from inside, there may be more light than we suppose. To our shame we have often expected very little of people as we see them descend into darkness, and have left them without stimulation from us, or any opportunity to find their own. Extraordinary research in psychology is showing that, invited to re-engage with the world, many minds that appeared utterly lost are in fact still living. Their reality may not be the same as that of most people, but it is still a living experience – and sometimes our worlds can reconnect:

My father had dementia. It wasn't Alzheimer's. It was memory loss caused by dozens of little strokes, through which some parts of his brain had simply died. Gradually over a few years he became more and more out of step with the world – prone to behave in unexpected and sometimes embarrassing ways. He remembered less and less: once, I phoned him while he was still at home knowing that my mother always left a phone on his lap, and he answered saying "I can't find my house." In consternation, wondering how far he could possibly have got in his wheelchair, I asked what he could see. He described... the back garden! I suggested that he turn around – and there, only a foot away, was the missing house. Gradually he became too frail to be cared for at home. He went to a wonderful nursing home, which he sometimes believed was his grandparents' home where he had grown up, and sometimes thought was a house we had once lived in – though there was no resemblance to either. My brother found this upsetting and tried, fruitlessly, to put him straight. I preferred to enter his world, and we enjoyed many a conversation based on his happy memories of things that had never happened! A favourite was his reminiscence of how he and I together had planted the hedge around the nursing home – which, of course, we had never done. Eventually he became so frail that he could not feed or care for himself at all, and often, could not recognise my mother, his wife of 60 years, though she spent hours of every day with him in the nursing home. He very seldom recognised me. Then, one day, long after he had stopped contributing much to any conversation, I was describing a favourite adventure from his youth, a story he had often told in his prime. I told the story, and he began to laugh. Then suddenly, he stared at me. "I know who you are!" He recalled a nickname he had given me as a child, not used for 40 years. I said: "I love you, daddy." He replied "I love you, too." And then was gone back into the dark. It was the last time we ever connected. He died a month later.[6]

Many people with advanced memory loss have moments of lucidity, moments of connection. They are a blessing when they come; a blessing for everyone. And what a blessing it would be if all of us, and especially those who care for people whose memories are fading, could stand ever ready for such moments!

It is right to do all that we can to nurture our minds, especially as they begin to fade. But in doing so, it is wise to face reality: to accept that there may be limits to what we can do to stave off decline. The most moving part of the film about Terry Pratchett was that, even while he was searching for a cure, he accepted that the likely end would be a progressive loss of his memory and the power of his mind. He was very far from happy about his situation! But he began to make plans for his eventual care. And in a programme on BBC Radio 4 in 2008, he described suddenly experiencing an overwhelmingly peaceful feeling that all would be well: a feeling that we would recognise as the serenity of acceptance.

The consolation of serenity is not the acceptance of a bad situation: in honesty and integrity, we must admit that the situation is bad. Rather, the acceptance of serenity is the acceptance of *myself*: the situation is not okay, *but I am*. Whatever the situation, I still matter every bit as much as ever. I am still as valuable, as worthy of love and respect. I am still precious in my humanity; precious in God's eyes. As has been true all our lives, we are precious in our human vulnerability, not in our perfection.

And perhaps there is even a spiritual blessing to be found in the fading of the mind. As memory of the past blurs and the ability to plan the future fades, our consciousness is directed very powerfully to the present moment. All that we know of dementia suggests that consciousness does remain in the present moment, even if in a reality different from other people's. As memory fades, a person may still lucidly engage with the moment – even though he or she has no memory of it a minute later. There can be joy in the present moment, even in the simplest of pleasures, and many find it. And the present moment is always sacred: God is in that moment.

What robs some people of their serenity as they face the challenges of memory loss is fear that they will be abandoned or even ill-treated as their minds become too frail to cope alone. That we should be prey to such fears is one of the greatest shames of our society! The media feed our fears, with stories of wicked carers or cruel nursing homes. But the press tell us only the sensational stories – stories made sensational precisely because they outrage our values. Good news does not sell papers! The truth is that there is another blessing which many discover as they become more vulnerable and dependent on others: it is that trust is actually very seldom betrayed. The vast majority of those who choose to work with vulnerable people are exceptionally kind and sensitive:

there are easier and better-paid ways to earn a living, after all! And in fact, many find a deeper love, given and received, a deeper sharing of the gift of self as they lean in trust on others as the mind fades: a love that comes from strangers as much as from family and friends. And offered to us all, always, is the love of God.

Consolation for a failing body

The older we get, the more likely it is that we shall suffer some serious illness or injury. It's not that our bodies are programmed to fail: it's that the wear and tear of living gradually takes its toll. Some are lucky and experience no real problems until later life or even old age. Others encounter serious illness much younger, even in youth or from birth.

Serious illness or disability is hard to bear at any age. It is wearying to be in pain, to be nauseous, to find every movement hard or impossible. Even the temporary inconvenience of a head cold or food poisoning can leave us wretched and self-pitying! It's a remarkable thing that many who face the noxious and enduring experiences of *real* illness do so with considerably more courage and grace than those of us who are merely mildly indisposed for a few days!

The consolations of serenity in the face of a failing body are as ever: to change what we can change, to accept what we can't, and to be wise enough to know the difference. And here is a wisdom which the seriously ill seem, very often, to grasp almost by instinct.

It is right to seek every possible means of healing our broken bodies and returning ourselves to health. We who live in privileged Western societies have the gifts of a medical science beyond the wildest imaginings of our ancestors, and beyond the financial possibilities of the vast number of human beings on this unequal planet. Many diseases that have killed millions, and still do in many places, can be completely cured. Even many of the diseases we most dread, such as cancer or HIV-AIDS, can often be stopped in their tracks, if not cured. Joints painfully crippled with arthritis can be replaced, and sometimes even hearts, lungs, livers, eyes – even ears can be made to hear again. It is right to engage the best that medicine can offer us (and to fight so that every human being can share equally in this bounty). But often, it takes great courage to engage this fight: treatment may be very painful, or involve unpleasant side effects which can sometimes seem worse than the disease itself. And still, not every injury can be mended, and not every illness cured.

What is it that gives some of those who experience serious incurable illness such good grace? Some of these people will tell you that they are graceful because there is no other option. As one young woman in her late 20s, let's call her Sarah, suffering from a chronic illness that had already robbed her of the ability to walk or work, said: "This is me. This is my life. I'm ill, and I'm only going to get worse – but I'm not going to be miserable as well!"[7] This girl was often in pain, sometimes too weak to do anything at all. But she was remarkably cheerful nearly all the time. And here, we recognise the serenity of acceptance.

As ever, the consolation of serenity is not resignation to a bad situation, it is acceptance of *myself.* Like Sarah, we go on working to change, to improve whatever we can in our situation. But we also have the wisdom to know that living in regret and anger, in unforgiveness and grievance over what is unlikely to be mended, will only add to our stress and take away any possibility of joy. We let go of those things and come home to ourselves. The situation is not okay, but *I* am okay: still as important, as worthy of respect and love as ever. The secret of those who cope so gracefully with incurable illness is this self-esteem: *I am not my illness; and I live in acceptance of all that I am.* And for many, it's not that the serenity of self-acceptance *survives* the challenge of serious illness: rather, they only discover it *because* they have faced that challenge!

Nancy Astor once said:

> I used to dread getting older because I thought I would not be able to do all the things I wanted to do, but now that I am older I find that I don't want to do them.[8]

This would resonate with many seriously ill people! We find that we cannot do the things we used to love – whether it be our work, or dancing, or even staying awake all the way through a film. But we find that there are other, unexpected compensations in our new situation. Some people do become embittered by long illness. But a surprising number find it enriching. One woman's words capture a feeling shared by many:

> Of course, when I first fell ill and was told that it was incurable I was horrified. All that I saw in the future was an endless emptiness of loss! But now, I have come to realise that many of the things that I thought were important were really very trivial. And many of the things which I never made time for before now seem to me to matter far more than anything else! My values have been turned upside-down – put straight – by this experience. If I could wave a magic wand and go back in time, I would not choose to avoid this illness. It has enriched my life and led me to a peace and joy that I had never imagined. I prefer life the way it is now to the way it was before.[9]

There are special spiritual blessings buried in the experience of serious illness. Most of us who face this become, to some degree or other, more helpless than those who are in full health. In that helplessness we learn to trust those who help us, and often discover for the first time the joys of such trust. But more than this, physical helplessness directs our attention away from the busy world of *doing* into the possibilities of the spiritual world of *being*. However helpless we are, we can still take the journey to spiritual fulfilment that we have explored through this book. The fruits of that journey are a blessing, not only for ourselves, but for all whose paths we cross. For example, Sarah lights the room up by her spiritual presence. The power of her being, the sheer peace and joy that shine from her affect everyone she meets. She radiates love, and touches lives.

What distresses many when they become incurably ill or infirm is the fear that they will somehow move to the sidelines of life and be left behind as the healthy carry on their busy activities. It is a sad indictment that some do experience this marginalisation: trapped perhaps in a deafness which makes communication too difficult for the impatient, or a slowness of movement which the vigorous find intolerable, or a sickroom which bores or frightens people with its presentiments of their own future. They are left in loneliness, abandoned by the thoughtless and selfish. But for many, serious illness opens up a new solidarity with others.

Perhaps the best example of this comes from breast cancer. So many women experience either cancer or a lump which might be cancer! All women, even the wholly healthy, are invited to attend screenings which may at any moment reveal something sinister. Somehow there has grown up a "sisterhood" of breast cancer: a network of women who support one another, share experiences, hold one another's hand through dark moments. At the core are those who have had the cancer themselves, but this sisterhood includes many others who are healthy: who wear pink ribbons, walk night-time marathons wearing their bras outside their shirts, or bake to raise money to support care for sufferers and research into the disease. Nothing makes having breast cancer a good experience. But the solidarity which surrounds this disease is an extraordinary sharing of the gift of self: a solidarity which, to paraphrase the advertisement, reaches the parts that ordinary friendships do not reach.

Such solidarity is not confined to breast cancer. Fall ill, and most of us discover that we are surrounded by love – even if we'd never noticed it before! As Jim recounts:

An old confrere of mine was dying. He was famous for his caustic wit and accurate diagnoses of all our failings. Two days before he died I rang him from California. He didn't want to talk about himself. He only wanted to praise all the members of the community. He concluded his long paean of praise with the words, "I never fully realised that I was surrounded all my life by such love."

When we are open to receive love, as he was at the end of his long life, we begin to see that the love was there all the time but we were too busy to notice it or to receive it or to be grateful for it. Strangely it often takes an illness to open our eyes to the love and goodness in others, in those who care for us and in those who are concerned for us and pray for us.

Sickness is not just a time of pain and suffering. Very often it is a time of inner enlightenment, great spiritual growth, and the development of profound trust in God. Pope John Paul II drew attention to this when he wrote:

> Down through the centuries and generations it has been seen that in suffering there is concealed a particular power that draws a person interiorly close to Christ, a special grace.[10]

As Jim recalls:

> When I said to a friend, Pamela, who had come through long years of sickness, that only those who have found Christ in their suffering can really understand this kind of language she replied, "Absolutely! But there is no other language to describe what happens to you when you really accept Christ in your sickness and suffering. It is Gospel."

Consolation as we face death

Why are we so afraid of death? For the unbeliever, death is a passage into nothingness, and what is there to fear in that? For the believer, death is a passage to a better life, united with the God of love, and surely there is nothing to fear there!

Why do we want so much to hang on to life in this world, with all its dissatisfactions and discomforts? As the writer Susan Ertz has pointed out: "Millions long for immortality who don't know what to do with themselves on a rainy Sunday afternoon."[11]

Sixteen hundred years ago St Ambrose, preaching at his brother's funeral, said, "deathlessness is no blessing but only a weariness if grace does not transfigure it".[12] Science fiction has explored the consequences of endless human life, perhaps most strikingly in John Boorman's film *Zardoz*[13], where a group of privileged immortals are rescued from their infinite and ever more destructive boredom by a barbarian who makes them mortal again. Philosophers such as Martin Buber have also explored the possibilities of human immortality and concluded that, actually, it is the fact that our lives are finite that makes them precious. Science concurs: nothing is infinitely rewarding. The more we have of a thing, the less we want it. The less we have, the more desirable it seems.[14]

If our human lives could stretch out for ever we would find less and less to value, more and more boredom and alienation. *How would you fill ten thousand human years?* For all their apparent differences, there are basic similarities across every human life, so that in living *for ever* we would be doomed to repeat ourselves again and again and again and again and again and again... To become a parent is an extraordinary, magical, glorious blessing! To parent two, three, maybe even ten children is a wonderful gift, though already, those coping with the higher numbers are starting to lose track and mention tiredness... *Could I face ten thousand years of parenting...?* Or would sheer repetition, in some base alchemy, transform this precious joy into meaningless chore? As with parenting, so with every other aspect of human life: never mind the tedious lows (the tax returns, the search for a plumber, the endlessly growing lawn, the unending problem of what to eat for supper). In ten thousand years of life, even the highs might well start to look mundane. Whatever Mae West may have said, too much of a good thing is *not* wonderful![15]

Our fear of death is probably not much to do with wanting to live our life on earth for ever. Sometimes it's more a fear that death itself may be unpleasant: as the comedian Woody Allen put it: "I'm not afraid of dying. I just don't want to be there when it happens."[16] But our regret that we must die is often really a regret that we must leave the stream of life, and leave those we love behind.

Dying can seem a lonely business. Even surrounded by people, friends, family, only I must die, while life goes on around me. The poet W. H. Auden caught that feeling that suffering and death take place in a mundane corner while the action of life goes on somewhere else:

> About suffering they were never wrong,
> The old masters; how well they understood
> Its human position; how it takes place
> While someone else is eating or opening a window or just
> walking dully along…[17]

We hope for someone to share our passing, to offer us gentle care. Most of us fear dying utterly alone. Many who commit suicide phone the Samaritans' helpline, and ask for companionship as they wait for the poison they have swallowed to take effect, reaching out for love even from a stranger. Soldiers dying in battle call out for the safety of their mothers' arms. We can all feel the horror of the nurse, Magdeline Makola, who was abducted, tied up and left to die alone in cold and darkness in the boot of a car over Christmas 2008. It was more than a week before she was found, thankfully still alive, and rescued.

Perhaps the worst pain in dying is leaving those we love. The sorrow is terrible and real: we want so desperately to be always there for those we care for! As Stephanie recalls:

> I remember my grandmother laying up small treasures for her children and grandchildren, to nurture them after her death. And Kate, dying of cancer in her mid 30s, creating living memories

through joyfully embracing each moment with her children. I see her dancing on Seaford beach with her three young sons, dancing on the very edge between land and sea; dancing on the very edge between life and death, her "pain-pump" hidden under her sweater. And in their shared delight, absolute gifts of self were given and received. In the evenings, when all was quiet, she boxed up memories for each son in photographs and letters and mementoes of moments shared: to tell them that they were loved, and each loved uniquely.

Letting go of those we love when it is they who slip into death is just as hard. This is the true context of Dylan Thomas' much-quoted verse, quoted at the beginning of this chapter. These are not the words of a man in protest at his own death. These are the words the poet wrote in protest at losing his father. They are in fact less a rejection of death itself, and more a cry of love.

What consolation can living in serenity offer in the face of death? It's right to do all we can to save human life, our own and others. There is an enormous courage in investing in life as strongly as we can for as long as we can. But to cling to life desperately, angrily, resentfully as we fight a losing battle to survive is a wretched experience which spoils the time we have left. To live in the joyful peace of serenity in each moment, even if it may be our last, allows us the space and the grace to enjoy the life we have. Any hospice worker can tell you that the end of life experienced this way is often rich and full of love given and received! Many even discover the joyful peace of serenity only as they near death.

Those who work with the dying know that there comes a time to let go of the struggle to survive. Many reach a moment when they are ready to go, and this is often a moment of great peace, a relief that is thankful, in which we recognise again the acceptance of serenity. And here serenity is needed, not only in the dying, but in those who tend them: the serenity to accept and respect the letting go in a final gift of love. Just the day before she died, Jim's sister said to her daughter: "I am sorry now to be leaving you all but the time has come for me to go back to God." Those were her last words. But what a gift they were to all her family!

Death may take our human embodiment, but it cannot take away our significance or value. A play does not lose its meaning when the final curtain falls, and nor does a person. Nor does the love we have for one another end with death. Many of the things which masquerade as love do end: the "love" that is really a selfish neediness, or that which is really possessiveness. But the gift of self which is true love, like any gift, stays with the recipient, forever present in the heart. And no one is truly alone in death, even if we seem to be. Every one of us must die, and there is solidarity in that – a solidarity which we understand when we live in the *mindful presence*, the compassionate awareness which is a key foundation for serenity. These consolations of serenity are as true for the unbeliever as for the believer. But for the Christian, serenity brings a more powerful consolation still.

For the Christian, death is not the final curtain. At the Catholic funeral Mass the priest says, "Lord, for your faithful people, life is changed, not ended. When the body of our earthly dwelling lies in death we gain an everlasting place in heaven." A great change has taken place, certainly, but the person we loved in life is not annihilated in death. The most consoling gift of the Christian faith, the basis of all serenity in the face of death, is to be able to say, "We believe in the Holy Spirit, the Lord, the giver of life" (from the Nicene Creed), and so we believe in life with God for ever.

And those who believe in the God of love know that love is the strongest power in creation: everlasting and timeless. Love exists in *kairos*, in God's eternal moment, not in the brief *chronos* of a human lifespan. In dying we move into that eternal moment, radiant in love which can never end or be lost.

And for those who believe in God, there is always a gentle companion:

> If God compel thee to this destiny,
> To die alone, with none beside thy bed
> To ruffle round with sobs thy last word said
> And mark with tears the pulses ebb from thee
> Pray then, alone, "O Christ, come tenderly!"[18]

The word consolation itself, as Pope Benedict points out, comes from the Latin word *con-solatio* which means "being with the other in his solitude, so that it ceases to be solitude".[19] It is this presence of the other that makes consolation possible. For the Christian, Christ is always present as we die, even if there is no human companion. The more we live in serenity, keeping our faith alive, the more open we are to the presence of Christ when we reach the end of our life in this world, and the more open to the transition of death. Many people have used the image used by Pope John XXIII at his own approaching death: "My bags are packed and I am ready to go."[20]

A well-known story attributed to Mary Stevenson captures both the doubts that can assail the Christian facing the great challenges of life, and the promise of Christ. It is called "Footprints in the Sand":

> One night a man had a dream. He dreamed he was walking along the beach with the Lord. Across the sky flashed scenes from his life. For each scene, he noticed two sets of footprints in the sand: one belonging to him, and the other to the Lord. When the last scene of his life flashed before him he looked back, at the footprints in the sand. He noticed that many times along the path of his life there was only one set of footprints. He also noticed that it happened at the very lowest and saddest times of his life. This really bothered him and he questioned the Lord about it: "Lord, you said that once I decided to follow you, you'd walk with me all the way. But I have noticed that during the most troublesome times in my life there is only one set of footprints. I don't understand why when

I needed you most you would leave me." The Lord replied: "My son, My precious child, I love you and I would never leave you. During your times of trial and suffering, when you see only one set of footprints, it was then that I carried you."[21]

A MEDITATION

Let us begin by centring ourselves: creating a space ready to reflect.

- Choose a time when you have at least a quarter of an hour to spare. Find a quiet place, as free from interruption and disruption as possible. Sit in a comfortable chair with your spine upright, your feet firmly on the floor, and your arms relaxed by your side. Close your eyes.

- Feel the tension in your feet and ankles, and let that tension go. Let your muscles relax, and feel the tension flow out from your feet and ankles to the earth. Now focus on your legs and do the same thing: feel the tension in your muscles and let it go. Now do the same thing with your hips, your spine, your chest, your arms and hands, your neck. Feel the tension around your jaw, your eyes; let it go and relax.

- Notice your breathing. Don't try to change it. Just listen to the rhythms of your body as you relax.

- Notice the sounds that come from outside and inside the room. And then go back to paying attention to your breathing.

- Sit quietly like this for a while. What is passing through your mind? Maybe there is nothing there except stillness. Or maybe you have some thought or image, or some emotion. Notice what it is and accept it; let it pass.

- Thank you for this moment, in which I may feel the absolute peace and joy of serenity.

- Thank you for my being.

- Thank you for the love, the solidarity shared with others.

- Thank you, Lord, for your presence.

- Accept and acknowledge all your feelings and thoughts.

- Bring your attention back to your breathing and relax.

- And then gradually return to the world.

Serenity is the spiritual fulfilment of our human life. A life lived in serenity is a life lived in being, a being which transcends all the pains and travails of this human life. How blessed are all who can truly embrace serenity! How much more blessed are those who, in the sacred moment, can find and live forever in the presence of God!

Thank you, Lord. Thank you, Lord. Thank you, Lord.
Hold me in your love
and
Never let me go.

THE INVITATION OF CHRIST

Stay with us in meditative calm and listen to the word of God:

How blessed are all who can truly embrace serenity! How much more blessed are those who, in the sacred moment, can find and live forever in the presence of God!

Sadly, many people refuse to think about the end of life in this world. And when someone does begin to talk about it, someone else is sure to complain that the conversation has become very morbid! And yet the favourite prayer of Catholics concerns the moment of death. We love to address Our Lady with these words, "Holy Mary, Mother of God, pray for us sinners now and at the hour of our death."

Jesus said: "I came from the Father and have come into the world; again, I am leaving the world and am going to the Father" (John 16:28). With these words Jesus gave us a whole new perspective, a faith perspective on death. He was speaking about his own approaching death, not as the end, but as his return to the Father. He knew where he came from, from the Father, and he knew where he was going, back to the Father. We can say that Jesus redefined the meaning of death for each of us. We can say, too, that we came from the Father and go back to the Father. As we have reflected in a previous meditation, "he chose us in Christ before the foundation of the world" (Ephesians 1:4). God knew us before we were born. God formed us in the womb (Psalm 139:13). We have come from the heart of God and we return to the heart of God.

That is our faith perspective as we grow older and approach the end of life in this world. It is this perspective on life and death which prepares the Christian to face departing from this world in peace and serenity. The prayer of Simeon finds a place in our heart, "Master, now you are dismissing your servant in peace, according to your word" (Luke 2:29).

Common sense tells us that we should prepare ourselves to face the journey we have to set out on at the end of life. It is not a journey that ends in annihilation, nor pitch darkness, but a journey that leads us into the eternal kingdom of God, into eternal rest. And Jesus makes that journey with us. In fact he tells us that he will come for us. He says, "If I go and prepare a place for you, I will come again and will take you to myself, so that where I am, there you may be also" (John 14:3). We do not make that passage from this life into the next all alone. Christ is with us all the way. In fact, he carries us.

A healthy spirituality helps us to face the final stages of life with peaceful equanimity. If we cultivate the habit of living in the present moment, of finding God in the here and now, in all the events of life, then, when we come to die, we will find God in the moment of death. That is why cultivating the spiritual life now, having a daily practice of prayer and reflection, is so important and beneficial. It guarantees serenity; it maintains equilibrium; it enlightens the perspective; it transforms the humdrum daily chores into moments of transcendence, moments of contemplation.

As you come to the last reflection of this book we hope that you are looking forward to many happy hours of stillness and contemplation in the years to come. God calls each of us to the fullness of life, especially in our final years. And Jesus says to each of us, "I came that they may have life, and have it abundantly" (John 10:10). The fullness of life is Christ's gift to us now. All we have to do is open our heart to receive it. Your daily practice of being still, entering into your heart, listening to God's word and saying a big thank you to God for the gift of life and the gift of yourself will ensure that you will have quality time with God. That will be good prayer time. That will be time well spent.

Notes

1   D. Thomas, *Collected Poems* (Blaine: Phoenix, 2000).

2   Quoted in E. Katz, *Old Age Comes at a Bad Time* (London: Robson Books, 1997), 87.

3   *Gigi*, 1958, directed by Vincent Minelli, screenplay by Alan Jay Lerner. *I Remember It Well*, Lyrics by Alan Jay Lerner, Music by Frederick Loewe, arranged and conducted by André Previn.

4   *Terry Pratchett: Living with Alzheimer's* (BBC2, 4 & 11 February 2008).

5   Attributed to American theologian Reinhold Niebuhr.

6   Personal communication.

7   Personal communication to the authors.

8   Quoted on http://womenshistory.about.com, accessed 26 May 2010.

9   Personal communication to the authors.

10   John Paul II, *Salvifici Doloris*, 26.

11   Quoted in E. Katz, *Old Age Comes at a Bad Time* (London: Robson Books, 1997), 87.

12   Office of Readings, All Souls' Day, 2 November.

13   Twentieth Century Fox, 1974.

14   This is known as Premack's Principle, after the experimenter who demonstrated the effect.

15   She is reputed to have said: "Too much of a good thing is wonderful."

16   Quoted in E. Katz, *Old Age Comes at a Bad Time* (London: Robson Books, 1997), 40.

17   W.H. Auden, "Musée des Beaux Arts" in *Collected Poems* (New York: Random House, 1976).

18   Elizabeth Barrett Browning, "A Thought for a Lonely Death-bed" in *The Poems of Elizabeth Barrett Browning*, Volume 1 (1853) (New York: C.S. Francis & Co.).

19   Benedict XVI, *Spe Salvi*, 38.

20   Quoted on www.bpjxxiii.org, accessed 24 May 2010.

21   Quoted on www.footprints-inthe-sand.com, accessed 26 May 2010.